McCALL'S
ENGAGEMENT
AND
WEDDING GUIDE

McCALL'S
ENGAGEMENT
AND
WEDDING GUIDE

by the Editors of McCall's
with Joan McClure

Saturday Review Press

NEW YORK

Published simultaneously in Canada by Doubleday Canada Ltd., Toronto.
Library of Congress Catalog Card Number: 79-122130
ISBN 0-8415-0130-0

Saturday Review Press
230 Park Avenue, New York, N.Y. 10017
PRINTED IN THE UNITED STATES OF AMERICA
Design by Tere LoPrete

Contents

Contents

Contents

Contents

Contents

Contents

Contents

Contents

Contents

XIII

Contents

Contents

Contents

Introduction

This is a book about the weddings of tomorrow.

It is directed, in particular, to the young bride-to-be of today, but it also deals with the special rules governing the wedding of a mature bride, a widow, a divorcée, and a bride of any age who has no close relatives.

It describes in detail the duties of the parents of the bride, the groom and his parents, the wedding attendants, and the guests at the marriage ceremony and the reception.

It provides step-by-step guidance to the traditional wedding customs and rituals, as well as to the legal procedures required in advance of any marriage, ranging from the simplest of civil ceremonies to the ceremonially formal wedding performed in a house of worship.

It also explains the striking modifications that our rapidly changing times are making in certain once-rigid social rules.

In researching this guide, we have made every effort to answer all the questions that might be asked by the members of the three families most closely involved in any marriage: the relatives of the bride, the relatives of the groom, and the couple taking the first step in establishing a new family unit when they become engaged.

This book is dedicated to all of you with wishes for a happy engagement, wedding, reception, and future.

The Editors

Engagements

Although some of our marriage customs have been drastically modified while today's generation of brides was growing up, most of the traditional rituals and rules remain unchanged for good reasons: following them is still the best way to make one of the most important events in a life as memorable and happy as it should be.

The same is true of the rules governing that practical prologue to a wedding—the official engagement.

Official and Unofficial Engagements

Today, an engagement becomes official when the bride- and groom-to-be announce their engagement to their parents. The parents will then tell the news to relatives and friends.

Announcement in the press has nothing to do with making an engagement official.

An unofficial engagement is not a real engagement in the social sense. The words *unofficial engagement* are generally used to define the period during which a courtship has developed into a positive plan for marriage but the date is still distant and indefinite.

A good example of the unofficial engagement is the relationship between college undergraduates who have been going steady since their high-school years but who do not plan to marry until after graduation when one or both are established in a career. Their feeling about each other and their plan to marry eventually may be no secret from their parents and friends, but officially they remain sweethearts rather than acknowledged fiancée and fiancé until they are ready to set the date for the wedding and actually announce their engagement.

THE LENGTH OF AN ENGAGEMENT

Experience has proved that the very long engagement is socially awkward and trying and that the very short one defeats one of the main purposes of a formal engagement, which is to give the pair a chance to see how well they get along as an acknowledged couple in many different social circumstances.

Especially if acquaintanceship has been brief, an engagement of several months, rather than several weeks, gives each time to become better acquainted with the other's family and friends and to learn to make some of the social adjustments necessary to a new couple.

In other words, an engagement serves as a trial run at working in social tandem. It gives the couple an opportunity to make sure that there are no major differences in background, standards, or temperaments that might make the marriage difficult.

An engagement generally lasts no less than three months nor more than six months, although there is no rule of etiquette setting a definite time span.

Sometimes, an official engagement lasts for only a few weeks for special reasons. For example, if the man is suddenly transferred by his firm to a distant post, it may be only sensible to cut the engagement short and rush through preparations for the wedding so that the couple can leave for their new location together. Or an engagement may be announced a year or more before the wedding is to be held. This might occur between sweethearts who want to make their status as an engaged couple official before the man goes off to serve a term in the armed services.

Under all usual circumstances, however, the length of an engagement is determined by the degree of formality of the wedding and reception. In most cases, three months are needed to complete plans for even a fairly simple wedding and a small reception.

Time must be allowed to consult with the clergyman if the service is to be religious; to make reservations and complete plans for a wedding breakfast or reception; to have invitations and announcements engraved and addressed; to invite attendants to serve; to plan and order their costumes; to get the documents required for the wedding license and to apply for it, to mention a few of the details.

A large wedding with six to twelve bridesmaids and ushers and several hundred guests requires about six months preparation if it is to go off smoothly without leaving the bride and her mother exhausted by the wedding day. It is very important to allow enough time to make arrangements for a sizable wedding and reception and to book dates for the caterer and musicians.

PREANNOUNCEMENT OBLIGATIONS

Quite often a couple will arrive at a decision to marry but will decide to keep the matter a secret for a while. They may do so because they anticipate parental objections and want time in which to try to win acceptance of their plans before revealing them. Perhaps they are not entirely sure of their feelings, and want to make certain that they are not merely in love with love before they commit themselves officially.

3

However, once they decide to share their secret, a couple becomes involved in a series of events that are governed by precise rules of good manners.

These rules are not outdated or simply "correct" customs; they should be observed because they are solidly based on consideration for the feelings of relatives and friends.

Telling the Parents

Both sets of parents should be told the news before it is shared with anyone else. The reason for this rule is obvious. Next to the bride and groom, the parents are the people most closely involved in the coming marriage. Only people too immature for the responsibilities of marriage would be so inconsiderate as to confide the news to their friends first. Moreover, although parental permission to marry is not required if the bride and groom are of legal age (see p. 91), the approval of the girl's parents is necessary before her engagement can be considered formally and socially official.

The young couple may tell their parents the news in whatever way they find the most practical and suitable. They may choose to tell their parents separately at about the same time. Or they may tell each set of parents together, in person or by a joint telephone call. If they decide to make joint announcements, the girl's parents are the first to be told; then the man's parents are informed with the least possible delay.

Telling Other Relatives

The parents will certainly spread the news through the two families and to their friends. This, however, does not relieve the young couple of the responsibility of getting in touch with their grandparents and other very close relatives, either in person or by note.

This long-standing rule based on thoughtfulness for others should not be ignored. Close relatives, especially elderly ones who have lovingly watched a young person grow from childhood, will feel hurt and slighted unless they hear the news directly from the prospective bride or groom.

Telling Friends and Former Sweethearts

If the engagement is to be announced as a surprise at a party, certain intimate friends are customarily told the secret beforehand. These friends are so very close to the couple that their status is almost that of a brother or sister. If there is no announcement party, intimate friends should be told the news in advance of any press announcement.

The same consideration ought to be shown to former sweethearts. Very often, another man is truly in love with the newly engaged girl and may be hopeful that she will become his bride, or another girl may feel similarly about the groom-to-be. It is thoughtless and cruel to let a former sweetheart hear of the engagement through a third person or a newspaper announcement.

ENGAGEMENT ANNOUNCEMENTS

There are only two ways in which an engagement may be formally announced: at an announcement party and in the press (see p. 29). It is never correct to send engraved or printed announcements of an engagement. The only announcements that may correctly go through the mail are personal letters to friends and relatives telling the news.

THE OBLIGATORY CALLS

Once the parents have been told of a couple's plan for marriage, certain calls must be made. These are the formal interview that the young man is expected to have with his future father-in-law and the calls that the parents exchange. The young man's call generally, but not necessarily, precedes the parents' calls.

The Groom-to-Be's Call

The day has passed when the well-bred suitor was required to seek out his sweetheart's father and "request the honor of her hand in marriage" before he proposed to her. The young man's formal call nowadays is no longer to ask permission to marry his girl: They have already decided that matter for themselves. The purpose of his talk with his future father-in-law is to discuss certain matters that are naturally the concern of any devoted father.

If his fiancée's father is not living or available, the young man speaks with her mother or other relative who stands in parental relation to her.

If a girl is marrying a man she has known all her life, and his family and financial status are well known to her parents, his call is only a matter of form. Under any other circumstances, it is only considerate of the man to report on his general financial condition, his prospects, and his future plans.

This conference with the girl's father is particularly important if the young people are still in college. They may not wish to postpone marriage until after graduation and therefore may hope that the girl's allowance will be continued until they get their degrees. No father likes to be taken for granted. He will continue his support much more willingly if he is allowed to discuss plans, ask questions, and express any doubts he may have. It then becomes his option to volunteer financial help if he concludes after the interview that it will be in the best interests of his daughter to continue to underwrite her education.

Engagements

The Groom's Parents' Call

The groom's parents always make the first call because the girl will be taking their name. Their call on her parents is their official welcome to the family of the bride-to-be.

This rule holds regardless of the relative wealth or social prominence of the two families.

If the two sets of parents have not met or know each other only slightly and live within visiting distance, the mother of the young man telephones the mother of his fiancée to make arrangements for herself and her husband to call.

The correct response from the girl's mother is an invitation to lunch or dinner at her house with or without the engaged couple present. In due course, the man's parents return this courtesy with an invitation to dine at their home.

If the two sets of parents know each other well, all plans for various family gatherings will develop spontaneously without anyone's bothering with the protocol of who entertains first.

If the bride's parents live in a distant city, the mother of the groom writes to them expressing her pleasure and that of her husband in their son's choice of a wife if she has met the girl; otherwise she expresses confidence in her son's judgment and their hope for the happiness of the young couple.

The man's mother writes a separate note of welcome to her future daughter-in-law if the girl also lives at some distance.

If the man is an orphan and has no older relatives who are close enough to stand in a parental relationship to him, his own call on his future father-in-law takes the place of a formal call from his family.

The Divorced Parents' Calls

If one or both sets of parents are divorced and perhaps remarried, the rules for calls remain essentially the same. There simply may be more calls depending on the relations between the divorced individuals.

When relations remain reasonably cordial between divorced parents, they put aside their personal differences to make the engagement and wedding as happy as possible for their child.

If it is awkward for the man's divorced parents to make a joint call on his fiancée's parents, each makes a separate call.

If the young man's mother is remarried, she may make the first call on his fiancée's parents by herself or her new husband may accompany her. However, if the usual invitation to a meal is extended by the girl's parents, the man's stepfather should be included in the invitation and he should accept.

The same rules apply to the man's father if he is remarried as well as to the parents of the engaged girl if they are divorced or divorced and remarried.

ENGAGEMENT PRESENTS

A wedding present from a relative, from a good friend, and as a general rule, from anyone who accepts an invitation to the wedding reception is one of those social obligations that is taken for granted.

Presents following the announcement of an engagement are not expected, however, except for gifts from certain people.

Even if the engagement is celebrated at the most elaborate of announcement parties, the guests are not expected to send an engagement present—and are certainly not expected to bring a gift to the party. If anyone does so, the bride-to-be should express her thanks, of course, but should not open the present in front of other guests. They might feel embarrassed for having come empty-handed, even though they have followed the correct procedure.

These well-established customs governing engagement presents are very practical. In any circle of young people, there can easily be half a dozen engagements within a few months. This means that each bride-to-be will have to buy a wedding present for each of her newly engaged friends. In addition, she probably will be invited to a shower for each. The strain on most budgets would be too great if an engagement present were added. Therefore, we have developed the sensible convention of concentrating thought and money on the wedding present and simply extending an expression of wishes for happiness following the announcement of an engagement, with the following exceptions. (All engagement presents are in addition to a wedding present, of course; they do not take the place of one.)

From the Groom's Parents

The bride-to-be will always find the engagement present from her fiancé's parents particularly touching and reassuring, as it represents a token of welcome into their family.

The gift is usually something for her personal use that will give her many years of pleasure, such as earrings or a brooch, an article that she might pass along to a daughter. The choice is not limited to this category alone. Family silver is one example of an appropriate choice for either an engagement or wedding present if it is suitable to the young couple's taste.

The groom also is usually given a present from his parents as a token of congratulations—a check to help with the honeymoon expenses or any other gift that will please him.

From the Bride's Parents

The bride's parents have a wide latitude in selecting an engagement present for their daughter. Their gift may be jewelry; table silver, china, or other items for her new home; or clothing for her trousseau. They often choose an engagement present of joint use to the couple—anything from candlesticks to a car—but they do not give an engagement present to the young man alone.

From Other Relatives

Other relatives are not obligated to give engagement presents, but especially devoted kinsfolk very often wish to express love and congratulations in a tangible fashion.

Their range of choice is enormous. The bride's Aunt Mary may decide to pass along the family heirloom silver teaspoons or to give her niece something for her personal trousseau.

The groom's Uncle John may bless the coming union with anything from a bouquet of roses for the bride-to-be to a check for his nephew.

From the Bride to the Groom

As a general rule, a girl does not give her fiancé an engagement present. However, there is no rule that forbids her to give him a gift after she has received an engagement ring or other present from him. Her best choice is an article that will be of permanent personal use.

From the Groom to the Bride

The engagement present with the greatest sentimental value is the keepsake that a man gives to his sweetheart to celebrate her consent to become his wife.

Almost always, his gift is the traditional engagement ring, but he is not limited to that choice alone. His engagement present may be any piece of jewelry from his fraternity pin to an heirloom bracelet, pin, or necklace. Or his engagement present may be a painting or any other simple and beautiful item that will give her pleasure.

Before the engagement is official, a man may not correctly give, or the girl properly accept, an intimate present of any kind. After the engagement, this rule is very drastically modified, but even then it is still not correct for a man to give his fiancée a major article of clothing or anything else that relates closely to her personal maintenance—if he observes the standard guidelines.

He may give her a car, but not a negligee. He may take her to an expensive restaurant, the theater, and a nightclub every night of the week, but he may not pay her apartment rent. He may give her magnificent jewelry or accessories, such as gloves, a handbag, or umbrella, but not a dress or coat.

From the financial angle, these restrictions are illogical. After all, why is a $1,000 fur coat taboo if a $1,000 ring is acceptable?

However, the rules concerning wearing apparel are long established and consistent. As a matter of taste, they are best observed.

Acknowledging Engagement Presents

The engaged girl is going to have to write scores of notes from the beginning of her engagement until after her wedding.

Good manners dictate that there is no escaping this duty. From the beginning, she should establish the habit of making prompt responses. She will endear herself to everyone concerned if she dispatches her thank-you letters without delay.

For sample letters and other details, see Chapter 4.

THE ENGAGEMENT AND WEDDING RINGS

Many couples prefer to do without an engagement ring and to put the amount they would have expended to furniture for their new home or, perhaps, to their honeymoon. However, by far the overwhelmingly large percentage of couples consider an engagement ring to have especially tender sentimental value, a token to be given and worn proudly as an outward sign that a life partner has been chosen. Therefore, selecting the engagement ring is, to many couples, one of the most important milestones in their romance.

The engagement ring is usually bought very soon after the engagement becomes official, though in some college circles the wearing of a man's fraternity pin is as much a symbol of an engagement as is a ring.

Sometimes, the investment in an engagement ring is postponed until an indefinite date after a marriage. Although most girls would rather have a modestly priced engagement ring than none at all, some couples on limited budgets prefer to postpone the purchase of the ring until the man can afford a stone that is now beyond his current means. Therefore it is not unusual for a wife to receive her "engagement" ring as an anniversary present some years after the wedding.

Choosing the Engagement Ring

Today, a man does not rush to the jeweler, buy the handsomest diamond he can afford, and present it to his fiancée. After all, since she is going to wear the ring for the rest of her life, it is a sensible practice for her to help select the stone and the setting that will give her the greatest pleasure.

Diamonds are the most popular gems for engagement rings, but they are not the first choice for everyone. Many women prefer the lovely blues of aquamarines and sapphires, the red glow of a ruby, the peaceful green of an emerald, or the beautiful violet of an amethyst.

Any stone, precious or semiprecious, or a pearl, is appropriate for an engagement ring. The choice is entirely a matter of personal taste. It is not the stone itself that indicates the ring's significance, but rather the finger on which it is worn. In this country it is always worn on the third finger of the left hand. A man's signet ring or class ring, cut to fit that finger, may serve as an engagement ring. The miniatures of class rings from military service schools, which are made specifically for use as engagement rings, are also suitable.

Many young women have a sentimental attachment to a

birthstone, which can make a lovely engagement ring in an appropriate setting.

JANUARY	*Garnet*
FEBRUARY	*Amethyst*
MARCH	*Aquamarine or bloodstone*
APRIL	*Diamond*
MAY	*Emerald*
JUNE	*Pearl or moonstone*
JULY	*Ruby*
AUGUST	*Peridot or sardonyx*
SEPTEMBER	*Sapphire*
OCTOBER	*Opal or tourmaline*
NOVEMBER	*Topaz*
DECEMBER	*Turquoise or zircon*

Buying the Engagement and Wedding Rings

If a man has inherited or has been given an heirloom ring, the problem of having to make a sizable investment may be solved for him. All he needs to do is make sure that the stone will please his fiancée. If it does, he should suggest providing a modern setting for the stone that his fiancée may help to select.

If he is buying a new ring, the practical and tactful procedure is for the man to consult the jeweler alone to make a preliminary selection within his means. When he returns with his fiancée, the jeweler will bring out only those rings within the determined price limit—usually including a wide range of sizes and settings. Then the final choice can be made without open discussion of the cost.

It is a good idea to select the bride's wedding ring and engagement ring at the same time because the two rings will not look well together unless they are of the same metal and are compatible in design. This is also a good time to select the groom's wedding ring if there is to be a double-ring ceremony.

The wedding bands do not have to be bought until shortly before they are to be used. Selecting them well in advance is, however, insurance against any last minute delay in having them fitted, engraved, and delivered. The jeweler, who makes note of the chosen designs and of the finger sizes, will be ready to complete the engraving when notified.

Since modern wedding bands are rather narrow, engraving usually is confined to the initials of the pair and the wedding date. The bride's maiden initials are used. If the rings are to be engraved, allow the jeweler a leeway of about two weeks.

By tradition, once the wedding bands have been selected, the bride and groom do not see their respective rings until the wedding ceremony. The day before the wedding, the groom picks up his fiancée's ring or has it sent to his best man. The groom's ring is delivered to the bride or to her chief attendant, the matron or maid of honor.

Paying for the Engagement and Wedding Rings

Frequently an engaged couple sets up a joint bank account to which both contribute to buy a house, furniture, and other major items to be used in their life together. These days, joint savings are occasionally used for honeymoon expenses if the couple wants a wedding trip that is beyond the groom's current means.

The sharing of some expenses is a sensible practice; however it cannot be extended to the purchase of an engagement and a wedding ring by any standard of sentiment, good taste, or tradition.

The groom always pays for the bride's rings, and the bride always pays for the groom's wedding ring if he is to have one.

Engagement Rings for the Widow or Divorcée

The rules for the first-time bride's rings apply equally to those for the widow or divorcée. She deserves both a new engagement ring and a new wedding ring. The disposition of rings from a former marriage is a matter of individual decision.

The major rule to remember is that the engagement ring from a former marriage is removed from the third finger of the left hand as soon as a woman becomes reengaged. The same is true of her wedding ring unless she has children. In that case, she may wear it until the wedding day whether she is a divorcée or a widow.

A divorcée ceases to wear her wedding ring after her divorce is granted unless she has children, although even in that case she may choose not to wear her wedding ring if she wishes to make her freedom to remarry entirely clear.

If a divorcée or a widow has a handsome engagement ring from her former marriage and wants to continue to wear it, she transfers it to the third finger of her right hand or has it fitted and perhaps reset for a little finger. Whether she continues to wear it after a reengagement depends on the feelings of her fiancé. If he will be disturbed by a tangible reminder of her former marriage, she should set it aside.

The Behavior of an Engaged Couple

"All the world loves a lover" is a well-known saying. An equally well-known fact is that the world finds extravagant demonstrations of affection boring and embarrassing. Even the youngest and least sophisticated couples are properly expected to confine themselves in the presence of others to a reasonable amount of hand-holding.

Dates with friends of the opposite sex generally end for the couple as soon as the engagement is announced, but this is not an unbreakable rule. An engaged girl may have occasional dates with male friends, alone or as part of a group, especially when her fiancé is out of town. Indeed, friends considerate enough to realize how lonely she will be when her fiancé is away will make a special effort to include her in group activities with a substitute escort. The same freedom is allowed her fiancé if she is out of town.

Once the engagement is announced, hostesses are expected to ask both members of an affianced couple to their parties, but sensible exceptions can be made. A hostess, hard-pressed to find a replacement for a dinner guest who has cancelled at the last minute, may reasonably appeal to either an engaged girl or man to fill in.

Today, the rules of chaperonage are so very much relaxed that they can be summed up in the comprehensive instruction, "Don't get yourself talked about unkindly." Engaged people are required mainly by good manners to act discreetly.

THE BROKEN ENGAGEMENT

The breaking of an engagement inevitably means hurt feelings and embarrassment for the couple and their parents. Everyone's unhappiness is minimized if details are not discussed and the news is told without recriminations or bitterness.

An explanation like "John and I realized that we weren't ready to settle down," or "John and Mary Jane agreed that they would be happier as friends than as a married couple," serves to inform people of a broken engagement in a way that saves the self-respect of both parties and does not force friends to take sides.

Press Announcements

If the engagement has been announced in the press, a brief statement about its termination should be sent to the newspapers that originally carried the story—after, of course, relatives and close friends have been informed. It should be addressed, as was the announcement release, to the society editor. Two standard forms are:

Mr. and Mrs. Hugh Stewart Jones announce that the engagement of their daughter, Mary Jane, to Mr. John Carter Green has been terminated by mutual consent.

or

The engagement of Miss Mary Jane Jones to Mr. John Carter Green has been terminated by mutual consent.

Invitations

If wedding invitations have been mailed, they must be canceled. The correct forms for recalling wedding invitations are given on page 168.

Returning Presents

The engagement ring is always returned, no matter who breaks the engagement. Other presents from the former fiancé do not have to be returned except for heirloom jewelry or family possessions. It is also customary to return love letters, especially intimate ones, to the author.

It is not necessary to send back small engagement presents or shower gifts. However, all wedding presents should be returned with a note from the girl. This requirement can be a chore, but it is always necessary. The accompanying note should be brief:

Dear Anne,

Thank you again for the good wishes that came with the salad bowl from you and Bill. But since John and I have broken our engagement, I must return your handsome wedding present. It is being sent under separate cover.

With love,
Mary Jane

If an engagement is ended by the death of the fiancé, engagement and wedding presents are not returned unless they are heirlooms of the groom's family. Silver, portraits, and other valuable family treasures must be returned so that they can be passed along within the groom's family in due course. If the engagement ring is an heirloom that has special sentimental value to the groom's parents, the girl should offer to return it. A new engagement ring and any other presents from the groom remain the property of his bereaved sweetheart.

If the engaged girl dies, her parents return the ring and other valuable presents from her fiancé and his family and send back any wedding presents that may have arrived.

TITLES FOR IN-LAWS

During the engagement, the couple does not change the forms of address they have been using to their future parents-in-law until the older people suggest other names. The girl continues to call her future mother-in-law Mrs. Green, for example, until the wedding. The man continues to address his fiancée's parents as he did before the engagement.

If the young people have known their future in-laws for many years and are on a first-name basis with them, they simply continue on that basis. After the wedding the bride switches to the titles *mother* and *father* or whatever titles her husband uses to his parents, and he does the same with hers.

If both happen to use the same titles for their parents, each one should choose some variation for the parents-in-law to avoid constant confusion.

Generally a solution develops naturally, although it is a sound idea for the young people not to choose cute nicknames for their in-laws. More than one promising family relationship has been chilled by a misguided choice of nicknames.

When in doubt, the only safe procedure is to discuss the matter with the in-laws and to abide by their suggestions.

ANNOUNCEMENT PARTIES

A party at which an engagement will be formally announced is always given by the bride's family. If the parents of the bride-to-be are not living, the announcement party may be given by one of her aunts, uncles, grandparents, an older sister or brother, a godparent, or a guardian.

An announcement party should precede the announcement of the engagement in the press. The correct release date is the day following the party.

An announcement party can be of any character—a luncheon, cocktail party, tea dance, evening reception with or without dancing, a dinner, or a supper dance.

Today, very large announcement parties are rather rare, especially if the engagement is to be comparatively short. Even in families where expense is no problem, an announcement party is likely to be simply a gathering of relatives and close personal friends of the engaged couple. There is no definite rule about this matter, however.

If a luncheon is the choice, it is held on Saturday or Sunday so that men can conveniently attend. Or, if the groom is out of town, the announcement party may be a luncheon or tea for women only.

If the home of the bride's parents is small or inconveniently located, the party may be held in a private room at a club or hotel or in the home of a relative or friend.

When a relative or friend lends her home for the engagement

party, she helps with arrangements, but she does not act as the hostess and does not receive at the door with the bride's mother. The mother of the engaged girl invites the guests, greets them on arrival, and, with her husband, assumes all the duties and expenses for the party, such as the refreshments, flowers and other decorations, music, and services. They arrange for restoring the borrowed house to order after the party. If a caterer is used, the girl's father pays the bill, including tips for barmen, waiters, and waitresses. If a cook or other regular employee of the owner of the house helps, she should be given the standard local fee for her time, plus a generous tip.

Sometimes the relative of an engaged girl will assume the costs of an announcement party as an engagement present to her. This is a particularly welcome gift if her parents cannot comfortably afford that expense in addition to the wedding expenses. If a girl's grandparents, for example, make this generous gift, they do not assume the roles of host and hostess unless the girl's parents are living at a distance and cannot be present. They contribute their house or other suitable place, the costs of the refreshments, music, and so on, but the bride's parents act as the official host and hostess.

Invitations

There is no one established form for invitations to an announcement party. The style is determined by the size and character of the party.

If the party is small with only relatives and intimate friends invited, the girl's mother telephones invitations or sends personal notes as she would for any other small party. The girl does not help in issuing the invitations, since she and her fiancé are the guests of honor.

For a gathering of more than about forty guests, making telephone calls or sending personal notes are not practical; some other form of invitation is called for.

The parents may write the invitations on their "informals"

if they happen to be equipped with these convenient little engraved notes. If informals are not available, printed commercial invitation cards with lines to be filled in are good substitutes. Today, these practical invitations can be used for virtually any festivity.

Engraved invitations are suitable only if the announcement party is to be a very large and formal dinner or dance. It should be emphasized that such formal invitations are *party* invitations. It is not correct to word such invitations so as to constitute an engraved announcement of the engagement itself.

If the engagement announcement is to come as a surprise to most of the guests, the invitations are issued as for any dinner, dance, or cocktail party and no mention is made of the guests of honor.

If news of the engagement is not a secret by the time the announcement party is under way, the purpose of the celebration can be indicated on the invitation by a line such as *To meet John Carter Green* or *In honor of Mary Jane Jones and John Carter Green.*

Below is an example of an invitation on an informal:

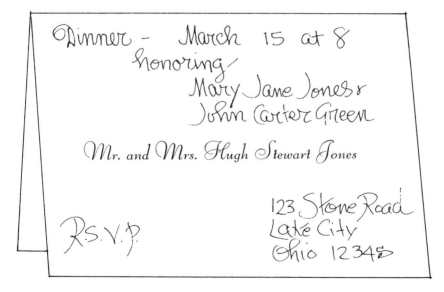

Telling the News

The announcement of the engagement at the party can be made in a number of ways.

At a small gathering, the bride's mother may tell the guests as she welcomes them on arrival, "I am so glad you are with us to celebrate Mary Jane's engagement and to meet her fiancé." Or the girl may receive with her mother and inform each guest of the news by displaying her engagement ring. Or the announcement may be saved until her father is ready to propose a toast to the couple.

Receiving Lines

At a large gathering, a regular receiving line may be set up with the engaged girl's mother, as hostess, nearest the door. Her daughter stands next; then the fiancé.

If the father of the girl is also in line, the usual positions are mother of the girl, the fiancé, the girl, her father. Usually, however, her father does not join the receiving line, but walks around the room making any necessary introductions to the groom's parents and other guests.

On occasion, the parents of the young man stand in the receiving line. This is a practical arrangement if they are not known to many of the other guests. Including them in the line is also an understanding and tactful gesture from the girl's parents. All too often, the parents of an engaged man feel left out during the prewedding festivities which are largely oriented towards the bride-to-be and her parents. Standing in line does not make the parents of the young man co-hosts; it merely indicates that they are especially honored guests.

If all the principals stand in the receiving line, the usual arrangement is mother of the bride-to-be, her future son-in-law, her daughter, father of the groom, mother of the groom, father of the bride.

If the father of the girl does not stand in the line, the positions of the groom's parents are reversed because it is customary not to leave a woman standing last in a receiving line.

Toasts

The toast to the future bride and groom is made by her father or, if he is not present, by her nearest male relative.

The standard procedure is for him to rise when all the guests have been supplied with drinks, catch everyone's attention, and say something such as, "Her mother and I are happy to announce the engagement of our daughter Mary to John Green, and ask you to join us in a toast to them and their future together."

All present, except John and Mary, rise and drink the toast (which means taking a sip, not draining the glass) and sit down.

John then rises and replies to the toast. Unless he is an accomplished speaker, his most effective response is brief. "Thank you for both of us" is fine if said with meaning. He may then propose a toast to the parents. Mary then rises, as do all but the four parents, to drink the second toast.

All the above rules for sitting and standing are proper for a toast proposed at a table. At a reception, many of the guests will be standing when the toast is proposed; the only convention to be observed, in this case, is that the recipients of the toast do not drink to themselves.

Champagne is the traditional drink for toasts on this occasion, but other wines are equally correct. A toast may also be drunk with punch, highballs, or cocktails, or with cider or non-alcoholic drinks, which are often served in addition to or possibly instead of champagne. A toast is not correctly proposed by lifting a glass of water, but a guest who does not have any other drink handy properly joins the toast by lifting a water glass. The important point is to join the ceremony of the toast by lifting one's glass—the beverage it contains does not matter.

ENGAGEMENT PARTIES

Usually there will be a series of small parties after an engagement becomes official, especially if there is no large announcement party.

The parents of the groom will want to introduce their prospective daughter-in-law and her parents to their relatives and close friends. The parents of the engaged girl will feel the same about presenting her fiancé and his parents to their circle.

Such parties usually have the festive informality of family gatherings and may take place at lunch, dinner, or in the late afternoon, depending on the size of the group and age of the relatives.

Good friends of the engaged couple may also want to honor them at special gatherings. If the parties are exclusively for young people, the parents of the bride- and groom-to-be are not included. However, if one set of parents is asked to an engagement party, the other set should be also.

Showers are a special form of engagement party that have certain rules of their own. (See the following section.) The parties that precede the wedding by only a day or so—bachelor dinner, bridesmaids' lunch, and rehearsal dinner—are dealt with in their own section beginning on page 176.

SHOWERS

The purpose of a bridal shower is to help an engaged girl collect some of the many items she needs for her trousseau and her new home. Its purpose is best served if it is scheduled fairly early in the engagement. Joint showers, given for both the bride- and groom-to-be, are becoming increasingly popular with many young people.

The Hostess

Anyone may give a shower except a member of the immediate family of the bride-to-be or her fiancé. This eliminates mothers, grandmothers, and sisters. Some authorities feel that aunts belong in this list, too. Cousins and godmothers, however, may sponsor showers if they wish. The reason for the restriction preventing close relatives from being hostesses is obvious: Anyone who attends a shower is obligated to take a present. Therefore, a party sponsored by a near relative is a virtual demand for gifts by someone too close to the couple for this demand to be in good taste. The maid of honor very often takes the lead in organizing and giving a sizable shower, but she is under no definite obligation to do so.

By tradition, a shower is supposed to be a surprise party. All surprise parties have inherent hazards. This is especially true for bridal showers. Anyone planning a shower should check with the girl's mother, if not the guest of honor herself, before making definite plans. Otherwise, the same set of guests may find themselves invited to a whole series of showers—an unreasonable financial burden on any one group. And an engaged girl may find herself with enough guest towels and scented lingerie cases for two lifetimes. It is the duty of an engaged girl's mother to keep the number of showers under control and to see that the guest lists are not extensively duplicated.

The Guests

Only those who know the engaged girl well enough to want to contribute to her personal or household trousseau should be asked to a shower.

Usually, the bridesmaids and the mothers of the engaged couple are asked, but this is not a standing rule. If the party is given by and for young people, the mothers are not necessarily invited. The two mothers are included, however, if someone of their own age is the hostess.

Anyone who accepts a shower invitation must come with a present, and, almost without exception, those who cannot accept send a present, in care of the hostess, to be opened along with the other gifts.

A main obligation of each guest is to enclose a card with her present, even though she plans to hand the package in person to the guest of honor. Otherwise, at even a small shower, the guest of honor will be hopelessly confused about the origin of a good number of items.

Invitations

The guests are invited to a shower in an informal fashion: in person or by telephone, personal note, or the convenient printed shower invitations available at card shops.

Even if *R.S.V.P.* is not written on a shower invitation, an acceptance or regret should be telephoned or mailed promptly.

A most important addition to a shower invitation is pertinent information about sizes, colors, and styles. The bride who has planned a yellow and white kitchen will not be delighted with a variety of blue, red, green, pink, and orange tea towels, canisters, and pots.

It is correct to suggest a price limit, if that seems sensible, by adding a line reading *$3 Limit* or *Not over $5, please.*

It is usual and very practical to limit presents to one category if several showers are scheduled. Among the more popular themes are:

Lingerie. Presents in the lingerie category are likely to be rather expensive. Pretty lingerie cases and small sachets are good choices for the less affluent guests.

Linen. Linen is always a popular and practical theme for a shower, since it affords a choice ranging from a double-damask banquet cloth to a tea towel.

Kitchen. The selection of gifts for a kitchen shower is very wide, ranging from an electric rotisserie to a bottle of silver polish. Pots, pans, wire whisks and other gadgets for preparing food, containers for storing items, spices, potholders, chopping boards, and cookbooks are always welcome.

Pantry. The pantry category offers a delightful variety—cookies, cakes, and crackers in tins, delicacies in glass and cans and packages, or items that will be useful when the couple returns from their wedding trip.

Closet. A closet shower is a good choice, since few people ever have enough handsome coat hangers. Every department-store closet shop has a good selection of them as well as shelf papers, storage boxes, space organizers, sachets, and perfumes.

Paper. Paper is another category with many possibilities at reasonable prices—shelf papers, scented lining paper for dresser drawers, paper aprons, flowers, table mats, and, of course, the invaluable paper napkins and towels.

Notes of Thanks

The guest of honor makes a point of thanking her hostess again, within a day or so, either by telephone or a note, whichever is more convenient and suitable.

A note of thanks is unnecessary if the donor of the gift was thanked at the party, but it is customary to write a "thanks again" note to anyone whose present was especially notable.

A note of thanks must be sent to anyone who sent a gift but was not present at the shower.

Office Showers

The character of an office shower depends largely on the size of the company or department and the number of good friends the engaged girl may have among her fellow workers. An office shower may be lunch at a restaurant or a gathering at any convenient place after work. The engaged girl's mother and bridesmaids are not generally asked.

It is not good business manners for the sponsors of an office shower to take up a general collection, soliciting everyone from boss to office boy, for a joint present. Only those invited to the shower should be asked to contribute to a joint present, or if they prefer, they may purchase their own individual gifts.

Joint Showers

Increasing rapidly in popularity are joint showers for the prospective bride and groom to which friends of both sexes are invited. Any item for use in the new home is an appropriate gift—desk and bar equipment, kitchen gadgets, books, records, edibles, garden and other tools. The only present that is in poor taste is lingerie. Gowns, slips, and bed jackets should be given at a party only for women.

The Use of the Word *Congratulations*

The use of the word *congratulations* is one of the firmly established rules of etiquette. Although the rule is explicit, so many people break it, with nothing but the best of intentions, that no dire meaning should be given to the frequent misuse of the word.

It is correct to use *congratulations* to a man when speaking of his engagement or wedding, but it should not be used to the engaged girl and the bride. To her, some such phrase as *all wonderful wishes* or *every happiness to you both* is proper.

The explanation for this distinction is found in the oldest romantic tradition of courtship: The man is to be congratulated on capturing the girl of his choice. To use the word *congratulations* to the bride implies that it is she who has been the pursuer.

Press Announcements of
Engagements and Weddings

Hundreds of announcements of engagements and weddings are sent to the society editor of every large newspaper each week. Since there seldom is room to print all the social news submitted, a selection must be made on the basis of relative news value. Obviously, a well-organized and typed press release is more likely to draw attention than a handwritten note or information given over the telephone.

The best way to assure publication of an engagement or wedding announcement on or near your chosen release date is to send in properly prepared copy in plenty of time.

PREPARING A PRESS RELEASE

To prepare a press release properly, follow the guide lines given below.

Use standard-size manuscript paper: 8½ by 11 inches.

Type your copy and double-space it.

At the upper left of the page, type either *immediate release* or your chosen release date.

At the upper right, type the name, address, and telephone number of the person submitting the copy. This can be the mother of the bride-to-be, a social secretary, the engaged girl herself, or someone else who can be reached, if necessary, for confirmation of the facts. A telephone number where the society editor can get an answer during the day and an alternate number in case the bride's mother is often not at home, should be supplied.

Do not send carbon copies. Have an original typed for each paper, or have reproductions of the original run off on a duplicating machine. Such copies are not expensive and are great timesavers. You may need several copies of an announcement if the two families are geographically distant. The news of an engagement or wedding will also be of interest in the various hometowns of each of the grandparents, as well as to college or trade publications.

Timing the Release

A newspaper release should reach the society editor's desk at least a week or ten days before its desired publication date. It is safer to allow two or three weeks for publication in the Sunday edition of a big city newspaper.

Although society editors will never break the release date, they are privileged to print the story at any later date as space is available.

An engagement usually is announced soon after an approximate wedding date is set. If there is a formal announcement party, the announcement in the press should be scheduled for the day following the party.

The release date for a wedding announcement is, of course, the day following the wedding.

PHOTOGRAPHS FOR NEWSPAPERS

A picture submitted for publication must be a glossy print measuring eight by ten inches. Every photographer is familiar with newspaper requirements; he will supply glossy prints at very little extra charge in addition to the mat-finished portraits suitable for personal use.

Attach the typed copy to the back of a picture, not to the bottom of it, so that you will not have to worry about picture and copy being separated. Do not type or write on the back of glossy prints. They are very easily bruised and may be unfit for publication. Type the name on a piece of paper and attach it to the back of the photo with transparent tape, being careful not to cover the photographer's credit line.

With an engagement announcement, identify the portrait:

> Miss Mary Jane Jones
> engaged to wed
> John Carter Green
> (release herewith)

With a wedding announcement, identify a portrait of the bride-to-be in her wedding dress:

> Miss Mary Jane Jones
> to become
> Mrs. John Carter Green
> on September 17
> (release herewith)

A picture of the groom is never sent in with an announcement of either engagement or wedding. If he is a prominent individual, the editor may request one after receiving the engagement announcement, or use a picture of the young man from the newspaper's files.

It is not correct to send in a joint portrait of bride and groom in their wedding clothes. If a newspaper wants a picture of the bride and groom on their wedding day, a staff photographer will be assigned to take it after the ceremony.

Pictures submitted to newspapers for use with engagement and wedding announcements are not returned, even if they are not used.

Details about when and where the bride's official portrait in her wedding gown is made are found on page 82.

Essential Items for an Engagement Press Release

A correctly written press release includes the full names of the prospective bride and groom; the full names of their parents whether living or dead; the places of residence (although not street addresses) of all persons mentioned; the schools attended by the bride and groom; their current business connections; and the approximate date of the wedding.

It is also customary to mention the groom's military service record; the occupations of each of the parents; the full names and places of residence of the grandparents; and any other pertinent social and professional affiliations of the two families.

It should be emphasized that the announcement is never made in the name of the engaged man or his parents. The bride's parents or other relatives make the announcement themselves or send the standard impersonal form (p. 34) or the joint announcement (p. 34).

The Standard Engagement Release

This sample standard engagement release is suitable for the young engaged girl whose parents are living and who is marrying for the first time. This form can be adapted to other circumstances with the changes indicated in the following pages.

Lake City, Ohio

RELEASE DATE:
Wednesday, April 14

FROM:
Mrs. Hugh Stewart Jones
123 Stone Road
Lake City, Ohio 12345
   Tel: 423-0709

OR CONTACT
Miss Jean Benton
   Tel: 799-4047

MARY JANE JONES
engaged to
JOHN CARTER GREEN

Mr. and Mrs. Hugh Stewart Jones of Stone Road (add Lake City, Ohio, if for an out-of-town paper) announce the engagement of their daughter, Miss Mary Jane Jones, to (*Mr.* here is optional) John Carter Green, son of Mr. and Mrs. Robert Nelson Green of Portland, Oregon.

A September wedding is planned.

Miss Jones was graduated from Laurel College last year. She is now an associate editor with Juvenile Books, Inc., of Chicago. Her father is the president of the Lake City Research Laboratories.

Mr. Green was graduated cum laude from Yale two years ago. He is now completing studies for his master's degree at the University of Illinois and will join Allied Computers, Inc., of Chicago in July as a cost accountant. His father is a member of the law firm Green, Brent, and Johnson of Portland. His mother heads the English department at Jefferson High School.

Photograph enclosed

The Impersonal Announcement Form

The impersonal announcement form is useful in many circumstances. It is a good choice when relationships are complicated by divorce. It can also be used by the mature widow or divorcée even if her parents are living.

The impersonal form follows the standard form in all general details. The main difference is that the announcement is not attributed to one of the bride's relatives.

IMMEDIATE RELEASE

> FROM:
> Give full name, address, and telephone number of person submitting the release.

Announcement has been made of the engagement of Mrs. Graham Bentley to General Mark Vincent Ellis, USMC. Mrs. Bentley is the former Elizabeth Ann Graham, daughter of the late Mr. and Mrs. Worthington York Graham of Palm Springs. Her marriage to Mr. Ian Briggs Bentley was terminated by divorce.

A January wedding is planned.

(add other pertinent facts)

The Joint Announcement

The joint announcement is often used by mature people, especially if the bride is widely known by the name she uses in business whether or not it is her legal name. Mention is made, however, of her former husband.

Mrs. Irene Gilbert, program director of station WQIN, and Captain Ronald Phillips, USN, have announced their engagement. They plan to be married in June.

Mrs. Gilbert is the daughter of the late Mr. and Mrs. Herbert Joel Allen of Los Angeles. She has a daughter, Mrs. Wilbur Morris Strang of Montreal, from her marriage to Mr. Lynn Fox Gilbert, which ended in divorce. (add other pertinent facts)

The Announcement Arranged by the Groom's Parents

If the future bride is an orphan with no close relatives or is from a distant country, the groom's parents may prepare the release. They should send it to the newspapers with their name at the upper right in case they have to be consulted for additional news. The release is written in the standard impersonal form, however, since members of the groom's family cannot correctly make the official announcement of their son's engagement.

> Announcement is made of the engagement of Miss Koto Osaki of Tokyo, Japan, to Mr. David Roy Blands, etc.

VARIATIONS FOR ENGAGEMENT ANNOUNCEMENTS

The names of both sets of parents, whether living or dead, divorced or remarried, must be included in a news release.

A Widowed Parent

If one of the bride's parents is dead, the same wording is used whether the announcement is made by the mother or the father if the survivor has not remarried. The word *late* must precede the name of a deceased parent.

> Mrs. Hugh Stewart Jones announces the engagement of her daughter, Miss Mary Jane Jones, to, etc. Miss

Jones is also the daughter of the late Mr. Jones who was president, etc.

or

Mr. Hugh Stewart Jones announces the engagement of his daughter, etc. Miss Jones is also the daughter of the late Grace Bethune Jones.

If a widowed mother is remarried, the mother's current husband joins her in making the announcement. Otherwise, the implication seems to be that she is a widow for the second time.

Mr. and Mrs. Reginald Barr Smith announce the engagement of her daughter, Miss Mary Jane Jones, etc. Miss Jones is also the daughter of the late Mr. Hugh Stewart Jones.

If a widowed father is remarried, the father's current wife joins him in making the announcement. Otherwise, the implication is that he has not married again.

Mr. and Mrs. Hugh Stewart Jones announce the engagement of his daughter, Miss Mary Jane Jones, etc. Miss Jones is also the daughter of the late Grace Bethune Jones.

Divorced Parents

If the parents are divorced but not remarried, the mother customarily makes the announcement. If their relations are reasonably friendly, the divorced parents may want to make the announcement jointly. In either case, the correct form of the mother's name is Mrs. Bethune Jones (a combination of her maiden surname and the last name of her divorced husband). If the divorced parents live in different cities, this fact is mentioned.

Mrs. Bethune Jones of San Francisco announces the engagement of her daughter, Miss Mary Jane Jones, to, etc. Miss Jones is also the daughter of Mr. Hugh Stewart Jones of Lake City, etc.

or

Mrs. Bethune Jones of San Francisco and Mr. Hugh Stewart Jones of Lake City, Ohio, announce the engagement of their daughter, etc.

If a divorced mother is remarried, the rule is the same for that of a widowed and remarried mother and her current husband joins her in making the announcement.

A divorced father's making the announcement is unlikely if his former wife is still living. It would occur only if the girl has made her home for many years with her father and has had little or no contact with her mother. It is still necessary to mention the girl's mother and her place of residence, however. If the father has remarried, his current wife joins him in making the announcement.

Mr. and Mrs. Hugh Stewart Jones announce the engagement of his daughter, Miss Mary Jane Jones, to, etc. Miss Jones is also the daughter of Mrs. Bethune Jones (or Mrs. Reginald Barr Smith), etc.

Orphaned Bride-to-Be

If the bride-to-be is an orphan, the engagement announcement is made by her closest relative: a grandparent, uncle, aunt, older brother or sister.

Mr. and Mrs. Perry Dwight Jones announce the engagement of their niece, Miss Mary Jane Jones, to, etc. Miss Jones is the daughter of the late Mr. and Mrs. Hugh Stewart Jones.

37

Widowed Bride-to-Be

If the bride-to-be is a widow, the widow's age usually is the determining factor in the announcement form she chooses. If she is very young, her parents make the announcement. For an older widow, the impersonal form is generally used even if her parents are living. Or she and her fiancé may choose the joint announcement form, an example of which is found on page 34.

If the engagement of a widow follows soon after the death of her husband, it generally is not announced in the press. If a year or more has passed since her husband's death, however, it is both customary and correct to announce the engagement of a widow publicly.

> Mr. and Mrs. Hugh Stewart Jones announce the engagement of their daughter, Mrs. John Carter Green, to, etc. Mrs. Green was Mary Jane Jones before her marriage to the late Mr. Green.

Divorced Bride-to-Be

If the bride-to-be is a divorcée, her age is the main factor in deciding the form of announcement.

If she is very young, and if she has returned to her parents' home, her parents issue the announcement.

For a mature divorcée, the standard impersonal form or the joint announcement, explained above, are the usual choices.

As a matter of taste, the press announcement of an engagement is not made immediately after either the man or his fiancée has obtained a divorce. An engagement may be announced quietly to family and friends immediately after such a divorce, however. The laws of certain states require a waiting period between the granting of an Interlocutory Decree and the issuance of final divorce papers. In such a case, there is no reason why an engagement should not be announced soon after the divorce is legal. It is never correct, however, to announce an engagement if a final divorce is pending.

> Mr. and Mrs. Hugh Stewart Jones announce the engagement of their daughter, Mary Jane Green, to Mr. Arthur Ellis Anderson, etc. Mrs. Green's marriage to Mr. John Carter Green was terminated by divorce, etc.

Divorced or Widowed Groom-to-Be

If the groom is divorced or widowed, his former marital status may be mentioned in the announcement of his engagement, but this is not strictly necessary. That fact does belong, however, in the press announcement of the wedding.

Separated Parents

If the bride's parents are legally separated, no mention of it is made in the press announcement. The mother is still Mrs. Hugh Stewart Jones. If the parents' relationship is friendly, they may issue the announcement jointly. Otherwise, the mother makes the announcement in this fashion:

> Mrs. Hugh Stewart Jones of San Francisco announces the engagement of her daughter, Miss Mary Jane Jones, to, etc. Miss Jones is also the daughter of Mr. Hugh Stewart Jones of Lake City, etc.

Adopted Bride or Groom

If the bride or groom is adopted, no mention of it is made if the last name is the same as that of the adoptive parents. If the name of the adopted person is different from that of his or her legal parents, the following form is used:

> Mr. and Mrs. Hugh Stewart Jones announce the engagement of their adopted daughter, Miss Emily Towar

39

Grant, to Mr. John Carter Green, adopted son of Mr. and Mrs. Donald Kent Bernard, etc.

Legal Change in Name of Groom

If the groom's name is legally changed, no mention is made of it unless those of the parents have not been changed as well. In that case an explanation is needed to avoid confusion.

Mr. and Mrs. Hugh Stewart Jones announce the engagement of their daughter, Miss Mary Jane Jones, to Mr. John Carter Green, son of Mr. and Mrs. Ivan Grenowski. Mr. Green changed his name legally.

PRESS ANNOUNCEMENT OF A WEDDING

In addition to all information included in an engagement announcement, a wedding announcement should give the full name and title of the person who will perform the ceremony, the name of the church or synagogue or other location of the ceremony, and the location of the reception. The full names of all attendants should be included, as well as their relationship to the bride and groom and their places of residence if they are from out of town. A description of the bride's gown and the bridesmaid's costumes is necessary, and other items of special interest may be added. It is not necessary to give the couple's destination on their honeymoon, but their place of future residence should be mentioned.

The release should be written for publication the day after the wedding. All of the above material should be submitted, although there probably will not be room to run the entire announcement. The editor will cut as much as she has to. She will also do necessary editing if the copy has to run a day or two later.

Lake City, Ohio

RELEASE DATE
Saturday, September 18, 1972

FROM:
Give full
name, address,
and telephone
number of person
submitting the
release

The wedding of Miss Mary Jane Jones to Mr. John Carter Green was held here yesterday (September 17) afternoon at the Community Church. The bride is the daughter of Mr. and Mrs. Hugh Stewart Jones of this city. The bridegroom's parents are Mr. and Mrs. Robert Nelson Green of Portland, Oregon.

Dr. Joel Meserve Moore, pastor of the Community Church, performed the ceremony. A reception followed at the Town and Country Club.

The bride wore a gown of (describe the bride's costume, veil, and bouquet). Miss Joanne Penn Miller, cousin of the bride, was the maid of honor. The bridesmaids were Miss Meredith Ann Willoughby of Santa Clara, California, etc. (give the relationship, if any, to the bride or groom and place of residence for out-of-town attendants). The bridesmaids wore (give a description of the costumes of the bride's attendants).

Mr. Jared Orr Thomas of Chicago was best man. The ushers were the groom's cousin, Mr., etc. (list full names, relationship, if any, to the bride or groom, and place of residence if from out of town).

Mrs. Green was graduated from Laurel College last year. (Repeat information, updated, about the bride and groom given in the third and fourth paragraphs of the engagement release found on page 33.)

When they return from their wedding trip, Mr. and Mrs. Green will make their home in Chicago.

The Paid Press Notice

There is no charge for an item printed in the editorial columns of a newspaper, but, of course, there is no guarantee that every piece of news submitted will be printed. A society editor has a limited amount of space and always has to select a few announcements from the many submitted that will be printed.

In large cities especially, many people do not care to prepare releases and send in photographs which may not be used, but they still want to share the news of an engagement or wedding with the community at large. Therefore they depend on the paid announcement column to ensure publication of the news on the date of their choice.

The paid announcement column usually appears in the Saturday or Sunday edition. Most papers will accept an order for a paid announcement by telephone and bill the client later. It is advisable to call a week in advance for rates, the closing date for the edition of your choice, and other details. Local newspapers can be checked for usual wording. The paid announcement is generally much briefer than the release prepared for editorial columns. The following typical examples may be expanded to include names of grandparents or other pertinent facts.

Engagement:

GREEN–JONES. Mr. and Mrs. Hugh Stewart Jones announce the engagement of their daughter, Miss Mary Jane Jones, to Mr. John Carter Green, son of Mr. and Mrs. Robert Nelson Green. A September wedding is planned.

Wedding:

GREEN–JONES. Mr. and Mrs. Hugh Stewart Jones announce the marriage of their daughter, Mary Jane, to Mr. John Carter Green, son of Mr. and Mrs. Robert Nelson Green, on September 17.

Planning the Wedding

DEGREES OF FORMALITY

Any type of wedding, from the most elaborate to an elopement, will fall into one of four basic categories of formality and cost. These categories are as follows:

Ceremonial

The ceremonial wedding is pageantlike, extremely formal and expensive, followed by an equally elaborate reception with an extensive guest list. The assistance of an agency specializing in management of wedding details is essential to the smooth production of this complicated social event.

Formal

Although similar in formality to the ceremonial wedding, the formal wedding is less elaborate and costly, with a shorter guest list, but it is still an expensive undertaking.

Semiformal

Decidedly simpler than the formal wedding, the semiformal wedding includes fewer guests. It may be followed by a large or small reception, or none.

Informal

The simplest of weddings, such as a marriage before a justice of the peace or in a rectory or church parlor, the informal wedding includes only a few close relatives or friends, though only the two necessary witnesses must be present. It may be followed by a sizable reception, or none.

Costs

Within each of these categories, there are so many variables that it is impossible to give exact estimates of costs that would be valid in all parts of the country.

Factors to be taken into consideration in making up a budget include the location of the wedding, the time of year, the number of people to be invited, etc., for example, prices for rental of space in clubs, halls, and hotels and caterers' charges are naturally going to be higher in metropolitan centers than in other areas. Since June and September are peak wedding months, costs are usually greater at these times. Formal wedding gowns can vary in price from less than $100 to over $5,000. Not only in terms of the gown, but for most of the details, personal choices can make the costs of two weddings of equal size and formality vary as much as 30 percent or more.

The best way to get a rough idea of what the costs of any wedding will be is to examine the chart on the following pages.

You already know, in general, which of the four kinds of weddings will best suit your financial circumstances and personal preferences. Get estimates from local florists, caterers, stationers, musicians, and other suppliers. Enter the amounts in the column headed "Estimated Costs." Then, to be on the safe side, add an extra 20 percent to cover tips, presents to attendants, prewedding parties, and the other necessary items that will come up later.

	Ceremonial Wedding	Estimated Cost	Formal Wedding	Estimated Cost	Semiformal Wedding	Estimated Cost	Informal Wedding	Estimated Cost
Invitations	Engraved.		Engraved.		Engraved or informal, depending on the number of guests.		Informal.	
Location	Before the main altar of a house of worship.		Usually in a house of worship, but occasionally in a garden, club, or hotel ballroom.		Small church, chapel, or at home.		Anywhere including city hall.	
Decorations	Elaborate arrangements of flowers at the altar and elsewhere. Aisle canvas. Ribbons the full length of the aisle. Awning and carpet from curb to entrance.		The same as for ceremonial, but aisle canvas, canopy, and carpet are optional.		None or simple flower arrangement for the altar.		None or, if at home, simple.	
Number of Guests	More than 250.		100 to 250.		50 to 100.		A few relatives and friends.	
Number of Attendants	Six to twelve bridesmaids. Two honor attendants for the bride (usually a maid and matron of honor, but both may be married or single). Best man. Ushers (the same number as bridesmaids) but always at least one usher for each fifty guests. (optional: flower girl, ring bearer, train bearers.)		Two to eight bridesmaids. Otherwise the same as for ceremonial.		Usually one but no more than two for the bride. Best man. Two ushers or none.		One attendant for the bride and a best man, or none, in which case strangers sign as witnesses.	
Bride's Dress	Elaborate floor-length gown with a train and long veil; bridal bouquet.		An elaborate gown, floor or waltz length; train optional; long or short veil; bridal bouquet.		Wedding dress of day or waltz length, short veil optional. More usually, a pretty afternoon or dinner dress in		Street or afternoon dress, no veil or bouquet.	

	Ceremonial Wedding	Estimated Cost	Formal Wedding	Estimated Cost	Semiformal Wedding	Estimated Cost	Informal Wedding	Estimated Cost
					any color but black. A corsage instead of a bouquet with the afternoon or dinner dress.			
Groom's Dress	Before six, cutaway. After six, white tie.		Before six, cutaway or sack coat with striped trousers. After six, white or black tie.		Dark street suit.		Street suit.	
Reception	Receiving line with announcer. Decorations: elaborate. Refreshments: elaborate buffet, semibuffet, or fully served two- or three-course meal depending on the time of day; champagne and other drinks; wedding cake. (Optional: individual pieces of cake boxed for souvenirs.) Separate table for the bridal party and another for the parents' party. Music: three- to five-piece unit for background music, or dance band of five or more pieces.		Receiving line, announcer optional. Decorations: elaborate. Refreshments: the same as for ceremonial. Separate tables for bridal and parents' parties optional. Music: the same choice as for ceremonial.		Receiving line optional depending on number of guests. Decorations: simple flower arrangements. Refreshments: small wedding breakfast or dinner, or cocktail-type food and wedding cake, or wedding cake only. Any beverages suitable to the food offered.		Usually none, but sometimes a sizable afternoon reception or buffet supper for any number of guests.	
Total Estimated Cost								

SETTING THE DATE AND TIME OF DAY

Even a small wedding is a more complicated production than most brides realize until they begin to make lists of all the separate elements. Orders for services, dress fittings, photographs, parties, press releases, presents for attendants, invitations, and scores of other enjoyable but time-consuming chores must be done before the wedding.

About three months should be allowed to prepare for a wedding and reception involving about one hundred guests, and six months are necessary to organize the details of a big formal wedding involving several hundred guests.

What Day Is Best?

Friday and Saturday are the most popular days on which to schedule a wedding. However, the long weekends involving Memorial Day, the Fourth of July, Labor Day, Thanksgiving, and Christmas are considered poor choices, since many people have other plans for those occasions and out-of-town guests must deal with the problem of heavy holiday traffic. Also, expenses can be markedly higher on these weekends. Caterers have to pay their staff extra for working on holidays; the client will naturally bear that cost eventually.

Certain other weekends are extremely popular for wedding dates. If you have your heart on a weekend in the following list, try to make the necessary reservations far in advance. Even six months in advance, space may be completely booked for the following dates:

> The first weekend following Easter
> All weekends during late May and June
> The first weekend after Labor Day
> The weekends before and after Thanksgiving
> The weekends before and after Christmas

Christian weddings are rarely held on Sunday, although they may be if the clergyman's schedule permits.

Jews do not marry on their Sabbath, which is from sundown Friday until sundown Saturday.

Important religious holidays are not practical, even if one's faith permits. Although there is no written rule on the matter, Christians traditionally do not marry on Easter, and in some faiths not during Lent or on any of the major holidays because of obvious conflicts with the usual holiday routine. Jews do not marry on the High Holy Days, but since these holidays end at sundown, an evening wedding may be held on these dates.

What Hour Is Best?

Although the time of day to select for the wedding depends largely on the kind of reception to be held, there are other factors to be considered.

A Catholic ceremony that includes a nuptial mass is generally solemnized at noon or earlier since that mass traditionally is celebrated before one in the afternoon. According to recently revised regulations, however, it may now be celebrated later in the day, depending on the parish.

A noon wedding is popular in all faiths. The reception following a midday wedding is traditionally called a wedding breakfast, although the meal is usually a luncheon.

Four or five in the afternoon is the most popular choice if the reception is to include light refreshments rather than a full meal. Six or seven is appropriate for a wedding followed by a dinner party.

Weddings in the south and parts of the southwest are often held about eight in the evening, especially in the summer. Evening weddings are held in other parts of the country as well if the reception is to be a dance followed by supper.

Consultation with the Clergyman

Once you have reached a decision about the size and formality of the wedding, choose a tentative date. Then, before making any other plans, either you or your fiancé should telephone the office of the clergyman who is to officiate and make an appointment to see him together.

Unless you plan to have a civil ceremony, this formal call on the clergyman has to be first on your list not only as a courtesy but for entirely practical considerations. The clergyman must first consent to perform the marriage service, and his church or synagogue must be reserved for a precise date and hour before you can order invitations, reserve the place for the reception, or proceed with the many decisions that lie ahead.

Choosing the Clergyman

There will probably not be any complications choosing a clergyman if both you and your fiancé are members in good standing of the same congregation. Several conferences with your clergyman may still be required, however. Clergymen of many faiths believe that a series of talks concerning the obligations and responsibilities of marriage is valuable.

Catholics are familiar with the rulings of their church concerning the marriage of divorced persons, but many people do not realize that the rules of some Protestant faiths forbid clergymen from officiating at the marriage of a divorced person in a number of circumstances; or that baptism of one or both members of a couple may be required.

Interfaith marriages involving Catholics, Jews, and Protestants present other complications, but in most instances these, too, can be resolved. Many changes in all religions are taking place. Some long-established church regulations are being modified and often abandoned as the various religious faiths draw closer together.

If you cannot be married in the church of your own faith, you may still be able to be married in a religious service. People of different faiths often arrange for two clergymen to officiate in a nonsectarian church, the bride taking her vows from one, the groom from the other.

Whatever the problem, ask the advice of your minister, priest, or rabbi, or seek the counsel of a local clergyman. They have dealt with a variety of complex situations and will know how to help you solve your problem.

Don't forget to reserve time for the rehearsal if it is needed.

The Visiting Clergyman

A wedding usually is held in the bride's regular church or that of her parents, and her clergyman performs the service. There are, of course, exceptions to this procedure.

If a member of either family is a clergyman, you may want him to officiate. Or if your fiancé and his family are especially close to their own clergyman, he may be asked to assist in the performance of the ceremony.

Such cases are not at all unusual, but they are governed by explicit rules of etiquette. First, discuss your wishes with your own clergyman. He will advise you about what can, or cannot, be arranged. If he approves your plans, he will send a formal letter of invitation to his colleague to conduct or assist in the service in his church. Only with such an invitation can another clergyman officiate in your church.

The Clergyman's Fee

The clergyman is not paid a set fee. The payment made for his services is considered a donation. The amount is left to the discretion of the groom and should not be discussed with the clergyman. If you are in doubt about the appropriate amount, discuss the matter with a deacon, vestryman, or other person who is knowledgeable about the financial matters of the congregation. The fee may range from twenty-five to several hundred dollars depending on the groom's circumstances and the size of the wedding.

If the fee is paid by check, make it out to the clergyman unless specifically asked to make it out to his church or synagogue.

The best man or the groom usually hands the fee to the clergyman in a white envelope in the vestry either before or after the ceremony; but he should never hand it to him in the church itself.

Church Expenses and Fees for Special Services

The purely practical matters concerning fees and services of the church should be discussed with the clergyman's secretary. It is quite inappropriate to take up such details with the clergyman himself.

Usually no rent is charged to a member of a congregation. It is customary, however, for the father of the bride to make a special contribution. He will be charged a small fixed fee for the janitor who opens and closes the premises for the rehearsal and ceremony. Nonmembers of a congregation can expect to be charged an established rental fee.

The choir, organist, soloist, cantor, and others who are regular members of the staff have established fees for their services. Ask the clergyman's secretary what they are and how to make arrangements for their services. Also ask whether a stand-by fee is charged if a personal friend replaces the regular organist.

Some churches can supply an outside carpet and canopy covering the sidewalk from curb to entrance, as well as a white canvas aisle carpet and aisle ribbons or silken ropes. If you want these items, ask the secretary whether they are available. They must otherwise be ordered from a florist or a caterer.

Church Regulations

Before making final decisions about decorations, music, and costumes, check with the clergyman's secretary about regulations. There may be limitations that will require you to amend certain plans.

For example, there may be explicit rulings concerning the style of wedding costumes, length of skirts, and head coverings. In some cases a veil for a first-time bride is required, although most often she has a choice.

You may have questions about the following matters: Are floral decorations permitted along the center aisle and elsewhere other than at the altar? Is a soloist permitted? Is there a restriction on the type of music to be played? Don't assume that "Oh, Promise Me" is acceptable in all churches. In some, all music must be liturgical.

Bridesmaids and ushers are never paired with each other in the bridal procession, and some clergymen do not approve their pairing in the recessional. You must inquire as to whether or not this is acceptable.

Make up your own list of queries as your plans take shape. If in doubt about any detail, do not hesitate to check with the clergyman's office.

DIVISION OF EXPENSES BETWEEN THE TWO FAMILIES

As with so many of our customs, the prescribed division of wedding expenses between the two families is now undergoing modification. Although the traditional rules regarding certain specific expenditures have not changed, there are many variants which are now acceptable.

The most important of the long-established and unchanged conventions concerns the reception expenses. The parents of a young bride are still responsible for the major costs of the wedding and reception. If their means are limited, their decisions about the expenditures for the wedding and reception must be respected. Even though the groom's parents may be financially able to assume some or all the costs of the reception, and might be delighted to participate in this fashion, they may not correctly do so.

There are, however, two exceptions to this rule. If a girl is a foreigner without relatives in this country, it could be difficult if not impossible for her to assume all the costs and arrangements for her wedding. In such cases, the groom's parents may quite correctly welcome their new daughter-in-law to the family, acting as if they were already related, by giving the wedding and reception. They might do the same for a young bride who is an orphan without an older brother, sister, or other person to act in place of her parents.

The second exception concerns the mature bride and groom as well as the young career couple who are financing their own wedding. Good taste demands that the bride pay for her own wedding dress and trousseau. For sentimental reasons, the groom should pay for her engagement and wedding rings, for the marriage license, and the clergyman's fee. But if they wish to set up a joint fund to cover presents to their attendants, a wedding breakfast or other reception following their wedding, and their honeymoon, it is their privilege to ignore the guidelines of traditional etiquette.

Expenses of the Bride and Her Family

The following two lists contain the *traditional* division of expenses between the two families. In recent years, several exceptions have become acceptable. These are explained in detail immediately following the two lists.

The bride's family pays for:

Her engagement picture
Party at which formal announcement of engagement is
    made

Fee for a professional wedding consultant, if employed

Invitations, announcements (see "Exceptions"), and postage

Her trousseau

The household trousseau (see "Exceptions")

Her wedding dress

Her medical examination required for the license (see "Exceptions")

Rental (if any) for the place of the wedding

Rental for aisle canvas, outside carpet, and canopy, if used

Fees for the sexton, organist, and soloist

Transportation for the bridesmaids to the ceremony and from there to thc reception

Fees for traffic directors and parking attendants, if used

The entire cost of the reception: rental of premises, decorations, music, the wedding cake and other food, beverages, caterer's fees, tips for service staffs

Photographs, including the bridal portrait, group picture of the bridal party, and candid shots or movies

Wedding present to the couple from the bride's parents

Wedding present from bride to groom (not obligatory)

The groom's wedding ring, if any

Presents from the bride to her bridesmaids, flower girl, and other attendants

Party for the bridesmaids (optional—may be given by them)

Rehearsal party (today often given by the groom's parents)

Lodging for out-of-town bridesmaids

Flowers:

    Bridesmaids' bouquets (see "Exceptions")

    Bride's bouquet and going-away corsage (see "Exceptions")

    Boutonniere or corsage for organist and soloist if personal friends (see "Exceptions")

Corsages for the bride's mother and grandmother (see "Exceptions")

Floral and other decorations for place of wedding

Expenses of the Groom and His Family

Engagement ring

Bride's wedding ring

His medical examination required for the license

Marriage license fee

Donation to the clergyman or fee for civil official who conducts the marriage ceremony

Travel costs and accommodations for the clergyman if he comes from out of town for the wedding

Wedding present from the groom's parents to the couple

Wedding present from the groom to bride (optional)

Bachelor dinner (optional—may be given by best man or ushers)

Rehearsal party (may be given by either family, but today most often given by the groom's parents)

His wedding costume

Furniture for new home (see "Exceptions")

Lodging, if necessary, for best man and ushers

Gifts for best man and ushers

Gloves for best man and ushers. Ties optional

Cost of the honeymoon trip (see "Exceptions")

Flowers:

Boutonnieres for himself, best man, ushers, both fathers and grandfathers (see "Exceptions")

Bride's bouquet and going-away corsage (see "Exceptions")

Corsages for both mothers and grandmothers (see "Exceptions")

Exceptions

Flowers. The floral decorations at the wedding and reception are the responsibility of the bride's parents, but they are not necessarily responsible for the flowers worn by the members of the bridal party.

In some parts of the country, it is customary for the groom or his parents to order and pay for all the flowers to be worn at the ceremony by attendants, parents, and grandparents, as well as by the bride.

On the other hand, if the bride's family is very well off and the groom's is not, the bride's bouquet may be considered part of her wedding costume and her parents may pay for it and all other flowers worn by the wedding party, including the groom, best man, and ushers.

Medical examinations. A blood test made within thirty days before a marriage is required by virtually all states, and some states require additional medical reports.

In all usual circumstances, the bride gets the necessary documents from her doctor, the groom from his, and each pays separately. However, if a couple goes to the same doctor for the blood tests, the man pays the bill.

The household trousseau. It was once taken for granted that the bride's parents would provide the silver, china, glass, household linen, and kitchen equipment that their daughter would need in her new home. It still is customary for the bride to collect most of these items before the wedding. Today, however, she very often waits until she moves into her new home to complete her purchases, since she will probably acquire a good portion of the necessary household equipment as shower and wedding presents.

Traditionally, the groom is responsible for the rental or purchase of the new living quarters and the furniture. This is another convention that is very often ignored today.

Either set of parents may make a wedding present of furniture, either new or valued family pieces, or may give the couple a check to be spent on furnishings for the new home.

And many young people, especially if both are employed, start their life together by jointly investing in both furniture and furnishings.

In other words, common sense, not unrealistic convention, sets today's rules.

Travel expenses for attendants. Bridesmaids and ushers are expected to pay for their own travel expenses, if any, but if the bride's parents suspect that transportation costs would be a burden for certain members of the wedding party, they may supply tickets to the place of the wedding if they are financially able to. The groom or his parents may do the same for the best man or ushers.

The bridesmaids' costumes. Usually, the attendants pay for their own costumes. The bride is expected to choose dresses that are within the means of the least affluent girl and that can be worn on other occasions. If the bridesmaids are to be dressed in period costumes that are expensive and not adaptable to later use, the bride's family is expected to pay for them. It also is correct, though not usual, for the bride's family to make a present of simpler dresses to the bridesmaids if they wish to do so.

Invitations and announcements. The circumstances under which the groom's parents may assume part of the expenses for invitations and announcements are given in detail on page 173.

Honeymoon. The wedding trip is traditionally paid for by the man. Here again, changing times are modifying the old rule. It is acceptable for a young couple to combine their savings for a trip that is beyond the man's own means if they wish to do so.

ATTENDANTS: THEIR DUTIES AND EXPENSES

It is a very special honor to be invited to serve as a wedding attendant. Since the invitation may not be refused except for a very good reason, the bride and groom should be considerate enough to give the matter careful thought and perhaps make some discreet inquiries before making a final decision. If travel expenses will be a real problem to a prospective attendant, it might be wiser to invite someone else to serve.

It also should be remembered that members of a few faiths are prohibited by the rules of their religion from taking an active part in a religious ceremony of another faith (though they may be free to attend the ceremony as a guest).

The bride generally chooses her attendants, and the groom selects his best man and the ushers. Very often, though, the selection of all attendants is a joint decision of the bride and groom and their parents.

Expenses of the Bride's Attendants

The bride's attendants are expected to pay for their travel expenses and for their wedding costumes which the bride has selected. In rare instances, the bride's parents may choose to make a present to the attendants of transportation costs and wedding costumes.

Each attendant sends a wedding present to the bride unless, as a group, they decide to give her a more expensive present jointly.

The bridesmaids' party, which is always optional, may be given by the bridesmaids or by the bride.

The honor attendant usually gives the bride, or the bride and groom, a shower, but this is not obligatory.

Expenses of the Groom's Attendants

The groom's attendants pay for their travel expenses if they come from out of town for the wedding.

They buy or rent clothes to match the formality of the groom's wedding costume. The groom traditionally gives them their gloves and boutonnieres as presents as well as their ties, unless the costumes are rented.

The best man sends a wedding present to the bride. Each usher also sends her a gift unless the group decides on a joint present.

The bachelor dinner is not an obligatory expense. It may be given by the best man, by the ushers, by the groom, or—as is the growing custom—it may be omitted.

Issuing the Invitations

The bride issues the invitation to serve to each of her attendants. It is not correct for her mother or anyone else to do so.

The groom issues the invitation to his best man and the ushers. In exceptional cases, the ushers may be invited to serve by a member of the bride's family. For example, if the groom is from out of town, he may not know the ushers who are going to be chosen from among the bride's relatives and friends. The bride's family will then issue these invitations.

When possible, invitations to the wedding attendants should be given two months or more before the wedding so that they will have sufficient time to make necessary travel plans and to arrange the fitting of costumes.

Replacing an Attendant

If an attendant is forced to drop out of a wedding party shortly before the marriage, another friend may be asked to substitute if there is time to have the wedding costume fitted. This is a difficult decision to make, however. Inviting someone to fill in can present a delicate problem because the last-minute invitation emphasizes the fact that the substitute was not the first choice. For this reason, many couples do not replace an attendant who must drop out, and instead rearrange the procession and recessional so that the tallest or shortest bridesmaid or usher walks alone. If the bride has only one honor attendant, one of the bridesmaids may be made a second honor attendant. There is no similar solution when an usher drops out, since there is only one best man; therefore, the odd man must walk alone in the procession. If the original plan was to pair the bridesmaids and ushers in the recessional, the odd bridesmaid or usher will look conspicuous; the only alternative is for the wedding party to leave the altar in reverse order of the procession with bridesmaids and ushers grouped separately.

An attendant should not cancel an acceptance to serve except in an emergency. The only valid excuses are military orders, grave illness, or a death in the immediate family.

THE BRIDE'S ATTENDANTS

The bride may have one or two honor attendants and several bridesmaids. It is not unusual to have two honor attendants unless there are more than four bridesmaids, though there is no binding rule on this matter.

Maid and Matron of Honor

The bride's chief attendant may be married or single. Her sister traditionally serves as her maid or matron of honor. If the bride has no sister of suitable age, she chooses a cousin or close friend.

If there are two honor attendants, both may be married or both single. If one is married and one single, the single girl traditionally is designated the chief attendant.

The chief attendant stands closest to the bride during the ceremony, takes charge of her bouquet at the proper time, is responsible for the groom's ring in a double-ring ceremony, arranges the bride's train and veil before the recessional, signs the marriage certificate as a witness, and stands in the receiving line at the reception.

The honor attendant also must be prepared for numerous other duties. She often helps to address the invitations and announcements. She arrives at the bride's residence in time to help her dress for the wedding, and makes sure that she is wearing the traditional "something old, something new, something borrowed, something blue." She reminds the bride to transfer her engagement ring to her right hand before she leaves for the ceremony, since the wedding ring must be placed first on her left hand. She takes charge of the bride's handkerchief if it cannot be tucked inconspicuously into the long sleeve or glove of a wedding costume. She helps the bride's mother by checking on the bridesmaids' costumes and distributing their bouquets before they leave for the ceremony. During the reception, she can be of special assistance to the bride's mother who, as hostess, cannot often leave her guests. When the time comes, she helps the bride change to travel clothes, sees that her luggage is delivered to the best man to be placed with the groom's luggage in the departure car, and at the last moment summons the bride's parents for their private farewell.

Bridesmaids

The bridesmaids may be married or single but should be close in age to the bride. She chooses them from among her sisters, cousins, and best friends. It is customary to ask the groom's sisters of suitable age to serve.

Bridesmaids have no specific duties, but they should be ready to assist with wedding preparations if asked. They often stand in the receiving line. However today's preference is for a short receiving line, and frequently only the honor attendants perform this duty, especially if there is a sizable number of bridesmaids. The bridesmaids supply the guests with artificial flower petals or confetti prior to the departure of the bride and groom. A primary requisite of the bridesmaids is to be on time for the rehearsal and the ceremony.

Junior Bridesmaids

Girls from ten to fourteen who are too young to be bridesmaids and too old to serve as flower girls can still join the wedding party as junior bridesmaids. They usually are the younger sisters of the bride and groom. Often there is only one junior bridesmaid, and seldom are there more than two, but there is no set rule about this. A junior bridesmaid stands in the receiving line at the reception if the bridesmaids do so. She is invited to the rehearsal party, but not to showers and other pre-wedding parties, although this depends on her age and other circumstances.

Flower Girls

Flower girls range in age from four to seven and there may be one flower girl or two. Traditionally, their function was to scatter flower petals in the bride's path, however, they rarely do so today. Carrying a basket of posies or a bouquet is considered enough responsibility.

A flower girl attends the rehearsal with her parents. They are all invited to the rehearsal party, of course, but usually the flower girl is too young to attend and must be taken home before it starts.

The flower girl does not stand in the receiving line, and if she is very young, her parents may choose to turn her over to a baby-sitter after she makes a brief appearance at the reception.

Ring Bearer

The ring bearer is also between the ages of four and seven. He may be the bride's little brother or the son of one of her close relatives or friends. He attends the rehearsal, but is usually considered too young to go to the rehearsal dinner and the wedding reception with his parents, although he is invited to both.

His main duty is to carry either a real or dummy ring attached by an invisible thread or a pearl-headed pin to a white satin or velvet cushion. If he is carrying a dummy ring, the best man detaches it at the proper time during the ceremony and pockets it before giving the real ring to the groom.

Train Bearers or Pages

Train bearers are boys between the ages of five and eight or slightly older. Since brides no longer wear excessively long and heavy trains, the bearers serve only as honorary escorts following the bride to the altar. They are not commonly included in wedding parties today. The rules governing the flower girl and ring bearer apply to train bearers.

Altar Boys or Candle Lighters

If candles are used at the altar, they usually are lighted just before the mother of the bride is seated. This service is performed by a member of the church staff. In some churches, the clergyman may allow young relatives of the bride and groom to light the candles. Boys of ten to fourteen are usually chosen. They are considered members of the bridal party and attend the rehearsal, rehearsal party, and reception, as do their parents.

THE GROOM'S ATTENDANTS

The groom always has one personal attendant, his best man, and several ushers. There should be as many ushers as bridesmaids—never less, though there may be more.

Best Man

The relationship between the groom and his best man is an especially meaningful one. The words *He was my best man* always convey a feeling of deep friendship. The best man usually is the groom's best friend or one of his brothers. If he likes, the groom may ask a relative of the bride to serve.

The best man usually is about the groom's age, but he may be older—the groom's father, for example, or an uncle. In any case, the best man should be a reliable administrator because, of all attendants, his duties are the most extensive. He acts as the groom's chief of staff in relation to the ushers.

If costumes are to be rented, he usually helps the groom find the right firm and arranges dates for fittings. Several days before the wedding, he checks with the costume supplier about the time and place of delivery—to individual residences or to wherever the ushers are planning to dress.

He should be ready to be of help in all other matters. If the groom has placed an order with the florist, the best man checks to make sure that the boutonnieres for the groom, the ushers, and himself are delivered to the ceremony in plenty of time.

On the wedding day, he arrives at the groom's residence in time to help him dress.

He takes charge of the marriage license (if it has not been delivered to the church or synagogue), of the envelope containing the clergyman's fee, and of the bride's ring.

He makes sure that the groom's going-away outfit is complete, that necessary items such as passport, tickets, and luggage checks have been included, and sees that they are all delivered to the place of the reception.

He makes certain that the groom arrives at the place of the wedding not more than thirty minutes nor less than fifteen minutes before the ceremony.

He signs the marriage certificate as a witness.

After the ceremony, he retrieves the groom's hat and gloves, as well as his own, and takes them to the reception.

He makes sure that adequate transportation is provided for special guests attending the reception.

He does not stand in the receiving line, but he may act as the announcer if asked, although this duty may correctly be assigned to someone else.

He proposes the first toast, which is to the bride and groom. If congratulatory telegrams are to be read aloud at the reception, he does so.

He dances with the bride, her mother, his own mother, and each of the bridesmaids.

After the reception, he helps the groom change to going-away clothes and checks again to make sure that he has wallet, tickets, keys, and passports.

He closes the groom's luggage and places it and the bride's luggage in their departure car.

He summons the groom's parents for a private leave-taking just before the newlyweds run the traditional gauntlet of rose petals, rice, or confetti.

He returns the groom's wedding clothes to the costume house, if they were rented. He is responsible for arranging to have the ushers' costumes, if rented, picked up and returned promptly.

Ushers

Ushers usually are about the age of the groom. They may be single or married. It is traditional for the groom to ask his brothers of suitable age, and those of the bride, to serve.

One usher for each fifty guests is needed for a large wedding. If there are only about fifty guests, it is not customary to appoint ushers; the guests find their way to seats unescorted. When there are several ushers, one is appointed chief usher to head the rest of the group.

On the wedding day, the ushers' duties are quite numerous. They arrive at the place of the wedding about an hour before the ceremony, and pick up their gloves and boutonnieres if those items have not been delivered to them elsewhere.

The chief usher checks to see that the aisle canvas, if ordered, is in place ready to be unrolled and that the ushers review their various duties, determined at the rehearsal, as they wait in the vestibule for the guests to arrive. (Details of the ushers' duties are given under "Seating the Guests," p. 192.)

After the ceremony, they help to transport guests to the reception, unless special cars have been provided for the wedding party. In that case, they escort the bridesmaids.

They do not stand in the receiving line at the reception, but circulate among the guests, helping the bride's father when needed.

They dance with the bride, both mothers, and the bridesmaids.

They help the maid of honor and the best man with the luggage of the bride and groom.

They help the bridesmaids distribute the rose petals, rice, or confetti. And they should be alert to thwart any pranksters who might have tied signs, tin cans, and old shoes to the departure car of the bride and groom.

Junior Ushers

Like junior bridesmaids, junior ushers are usually young relatives of the bride and groom. Their duties are the same as those of adult ushers.

Junior ushers usually are in their middle teens, though younger boys are often appointed. The problem of costume arises if the boys are under eighteen. A young boy does not properly wear either formal day clothes or white tie. For the correct choices, see "Clothes for the Wedding" (p. 68).

Clothes for the Wedding

The degree of formality of a wedding and reception, where they will be held, the hour of the day, and the season of the year determine the type of clothes to be worn by the wedding party and the guests.

The most important rule concerning the costumes for all the principals in a wedding party is *Be consistent*. If the bride is to wear a very formal wedding gown with a train and long veil, the groom, best man, and ushers must wear costumes of matching formality.

For a comparison of clothes appropriately worn at ceremonial, formal, semiformal, and informal weddings, see the chart on pages 46 and 47. Rules governing the costumes of the parents and of guests are discussed on pages 75 and 76 in this chapter.

The Wedding Dress and Accessories

Fashions change, but certain traditional aspects of the formal wedding gown remain the same.

Only a first-time bride wears a veil and an all-white wedding gown. Her groom's former marital status, though he may be widowed or several times divorced, does not affect this rule.

However, it is never correct for a bride to wear a white wedding gown and veil at a marriage held at a city hall, in a judge's chambers, or other business offices. In this case, the bride and groom both wear street clothes, and the bride wears a corsage rather than carrying a bouquet.

White, oyster white, pale cream, or ivory are first choices with young brides, although occasionally a pale pastel shade is selected for a classically cut formal wedding dress.

A first-time bride over thirty years old usually does not choose an all-white wedding costume, though she may do so if she wishes. Even if it is her first marriage, a mature bride usually chooses a beautiful cocktail or dinner dress rather than a long, sweeping, white gown and veil.

A wedding gown may be of any material, including satin, taffeta, brocade, lace, velvet, chiffon, tulle, organdy, lawn, or dotted swiss, that is suitable to the time of year and the climate.

It may be long, waltz length, or shorter; bridal salons are now showing pantsuits in elegant white silks, brocades, satins, and velvets.

The heirloom wedding gown always adds a charming sentimental note to a wedding, but it does create the problem of selecting bridesmaids' costumes that look well with it. It is the bride's prerogative, of course, whether to wear the beautiful, quaint period dress made for her mother or grandmother or a new gown of modern design.

The skirt of a wedding dress of any length should be cut generously so that it will fall gracefully if the ceremony calls for kneeling and afford freedom of movement in the procession to the altar and in the recessional.

Necklines are cut modestly high. An off-shoulder or strapless dress is not suitable to a religious ceremony, even if held elsewhere than in a house of worship.

Gloves. In some faiths, either long sleeves or shoulder-length gloves with a sleeveless dress are required. In others, cap sleeves without gloves are approved. If in doubt about this or any detail of a wedding costume, your clergyman's office will give you the answer.

A bride does not wear gloves if her dress has sleeves to the wrist. If she is wearing shoulder-length gloves, she does not remove them during the ceremony, since they are considered part of her gown on this occasion. Instead, the underseam of the ring finger of her left glove is opened so that she may free her finger easily when the time comes to accept the wedding ring.

A bride in street, afternoon, or dinner dress always removes her gloves before the ceremony begins and lays them aside with her purse, usually in the vestry of the church or synagogue or in a room that has been provided for the bridal party.

Headdresses. A veil, long or short, is a dramatic and lovely part of a formal wedding costume, but many brides prefer a chaplet of pearls, a circle of white flowers, or other type of headdress without a veil. Unless a face veil is a religious requirement, the bride is not obliged to wear one with a formal wedding gown.

It is important to choose a veil that will look well with your hair-do. Have your hair done the way you plan to wear it on your wedding day when you are selecting a veil.

Managing a veil can be a tricky matter. Try to have a private rehearsal with the attendant who will assist during the ceremony in lifting and folding it back or possibly detaching a face veil from the rest of the headdress.

Shoes. Slippers should match the formal wedding gown in shade—white or off-white. They may be of silk or satin, or covered in the material of the gown.

Wedding slippers usually do not have exceedingly high heels for two reasons: It is far easier to accomplish the stately, slow pace of the procession in lower heels, and to stand up for the considerable time necessary during the receiving line and afterwards at the reception.

Jewelry. With a formal wedding gown, simple jewelry is the usual choice. A strand of pearls is the classic ornament. The bride often wears no jewelry other than her engagement ring (which she transfers before the ceremony to her right hand), especially if the neckline of her gown is heavily ornamented.

Good luck items. The wearing of something old, something new, something borrowed, something blue, and a silver sixpence in your shoe is supposed to assure a happy future. A bright new penny or dime serves American brides as a substitute for the sixpence.

Bouquets. The size and shape of the bouquet is determined by the style of the wedding gown. The bride may carry a white prayer book, if she prefers, with or without flower-decorated ribbons. See "Flowers for the Bouquets," page 87.

When to order the wedding gown. The wedding gown should be finished approximately six weeks before the wedding day if you plan to send formal wedding portraits to the newspapers. If you allow less time, the photographer may not be able to process the portraits so that they can be sent to the newspapers at least two weeks before the wedding. Allow sufficient time before then to order the gown and to have several fittings, of course.

Fittings. If the gown is to fit properly, it is essential for the bride to wear the undergarments she will wear on her wedding day to all fittings. She should also wear either her wedding slippers or other shoes with heels of the same height.

The Bridesmaids' Costumes

The bride usually discusses the general theme and color scheme of her wedding with her parents and friends, but the final decision about the attendants' dresses is hers alone. She should make every effort to select a model that the least affluent of her bridesmaids can afford in a color that will be becoming to all. She should also choose a dress that, with a few alterations—the removal of sleeves or a change in length, for example—can be worn again. If she wants her attendants to wear period costumes that are not adaptable to further use, she should be prepared to pay for them herself. Of course, the attendants' dresses should be compatible with her wedding gown. If her costume is of luxurious white velvet, she would not select ruffled dotted swiss dresses for her bridesmaids. There are obvious advantages to ordering all the dresses from one bridal salon. (See "Bridal Bureaus," p. 78.)

Bridesmaids' dresses are generally the same color. The dresses of the maid and matron of honor may be the same as those of the bridesmaids or in slightly different shades of the same color. If there is a large group of bridesmaids, dresses ranging in color can be most effective. Pairs may be dressed in a color varying from pale pink to rose, for example. Or pairs may be dressed in several pastel shades—the leading pair in pale pink, the next pair in lavender, the next in yellow, and so on.

Although an all-white wedding can be dramatic, it is seldom the best choice unless all the bride's attendants are so young that the bride will stand out among them by virtue of her height. Colored accessories, such as sashes, headdresses, and bouquets, are usual for bridesmaids in white dresses. The bridesmaids' gowns should complement the bride's gown, but they do not have to match it in length. Waltz length or slightly shorter skirts of some fullness are popular because they afford grace and freedom of motion and add stateliness and drama to the procession. They are suitable even if the bride is wearing a floor-length gown.

Gloves. The bridesmaids usually wear gloves, but it is not obligatory that they do so, even if the bride is wearing them. They may be very short or shoulder length, according to the bride's choice.

Headdresses. A ribbon bow, a hair band, or a circle of flowers are the usual choices for headdresses. Artificial flowers are never suitable for bouquets, but they are both practical and correct for headdresses. Fresh flowers may be used, but their hazards are obvious.

Jewelry. The simplest jewelry, if any, is the best choice—a single strand of pearls or a gold chain and locket are the classic necklaces, worn with or without earrings.

Shoes. It is customary for slippers to match the dress in color. The best way to assure uniform color is for the bride to ask each attendant to buy her own plain opera pumps in white silk or satin and then arrange for all the slippers to be tinted at the same time.

Junior Bridesmaids

Junior bridesmaids look best in dresses that are identical in cut with those of the bridesmaids, although they may be of a different color or shade. If the manufacturer cannot supply the model selected for the bridesmaids in small sizes, the bridal consultant may be able to order extra material in the same color and arrange for a seamstress to create costumes similar in cut for the younger girls.

Flower Girls

If the design is suitable, the flower girl may wear a copy of the bridesmaids' costumes. More often she looks best if she wears a pretty dress suitable to her age. It may be all white or a pastel color. White socks, white strapped slippers, a circle of flowers for her hair, and her basket of posies complete her costume.

Ring Bearers and Pages

It is not correct to dress a little boy in a miniature cutaway, tails, or dinner suit to match the costume of the groom. The ring bearer's costume usually is a white suit with short pants or short white pants worn with a ruffled white blouse, a colored sash, socks, and strapped patent leather shoes which may be either black or white. Page boys, though slightly older, are generally dressed like the ring bearer.

Men in the Bridal Party

The formality of the bride's gown and the time of day determine the formality of the clothes of the groom, the best man, the ushers, and the bride's father.

It is of major importance that the clothes of the men who join in the procession be of the same character. If the groom is in white tie, the best man, the ushers, and the bride's father should be also. Their clothes need not be identical in minor details, but they must correspond in the degree of formality.

Today, with very few exceptions, the male members of a bridal party rent cutaways. It is also customary for men who do not already own tails or dinner jackets to rent them.

The groom or his father or mother or his best man investigates local costume-rental firms and places the order with the company for all the necessary costumes. The only way to ensure service and reliable delivery is for the costumes to be ordered from one firm well in advance of the wedding date. The outfitter will set up fittings to suit everyone's convenience. He will also supply size slips to be sent to men who live out of town so that their costumes can be altered and ready when they arrive for the wedding. The measurements for size slips should be taken by a professional tailor. The size slips should then be returned as promptly as possible to the groom or best man.

The best man should be delegated to see that the clothes are delivered to the correct addresses by a specified time; he should check on their arrival, making sure that each costume is complete as ordered. He usually takes charge of collecting the costumes and returning them to the renting concern. Each usher pays the rental and alteration charges for his own clothes and reimburses the best man, head usher, or other person who is coordinating the rental.

Junior Ushers

If the ushers are wearing either formal daytime clothes or white tie, it is best to dispense with junior ushers. Since a boy under eighteen cannot correctly wear either a cutaway or tails, he will be conspicuous by his difference in dress during the procession and ceremony. If a junior usher is to serve, he wears a dark suit in the daytime or, if he is past fourteen, a dinner jacket in the evening.

The Parents

The two mothers will need to confer about the general style and colors of their costumes unless the reception is to be very small and informal.

The mother of the bride selects her costume first. The groom's mother then chooses a dress that will be compatible in color, design, and degree of formality, since she will stand beside the bride's mother in the receiving line. One mother in a long dress and the other in a short one or in a shade that clashes puts both mothers at a disadvantage.

The mother of the bride should select her dress as soon as possible after the color scheme for the bridesmaids' dresses is chosen so that the groom's mother will have sufficient time to shop for a dress or have one made.

Once the bride's mother has chosen her dress, she shows it or describes its fabric, color, and length to the groom's mother. If she lives far away, it is helpful for the bride's mother to send her a swatch of her own dress material, as well as one of the bridesmaids'. In this way the groom's mother can choose her dress color and fabric with confidence.

If the bride's father is to escort her up the aisle, he dresses to match the groom in formality. The father of the groom usually does also, but since he is not part of the bridal procession (except in some Jewish ceremonies), he is not under the same obligation to dress formally as is the father of the bride.

Mourning Dress at a Wedding

Today, very few people wear formal mourning dress after a death in their family, but the rule concerning such clothing and weddings is clear.

The costumes of the bridal party are considered a uniform. A bridesmaid who is wearing the black of mourning in daily life must either decline the invitation to serve or agree to wear

75

the costume chosen for the bridesmaids. A best man or usher removes his black armband for the wedding.

The bride never wears black if she observes the rules. Neither do either of the mothers. If an unexpected death of a member of either the bride's or groom's immediate family occurs shortly before a formal wedding, it is either postponed or held on schedule with only the closest relatives and friends in attendance.

Wedding guests. A recently bereaved person will very often attend a wedding, especially if it is a religious service. If she is in full mourning, she should add some touches of white, lavender, or gray to her black costume. A male guest need not remove his black armband if he is wearing one at the time of the wedding. A person who has suffered a recent bereavement rarely goes on to a wedding reception, whether he or she is wearing mourning or not, since a mood of personal sorrow is not appropriate to the celebratory spirit of the party.

Guests

A woman guest may wear any color costume she likes. She would, of course, not wear an all-white costume if the bride is wearing one. She generally chooses any color except black, but she may wear a dressy black suit, if she chooses a pretty and colorful hat or other accessory to go with it.

As a general rule, women wear some kind of headdress at a church wedding. Today, however, the custom is no longer faithfully observed. Quite often, women guests arrive at a formal wedding without even a token headdress. A guest who is unable to check with a member of the congregation about local protocol can always bring a small triangle of lace, preferably the color of her hair or dress, to serve as a head covering if she would be conspicuous otherwise.

Guests are under no obligation to wear clothes of the same formality as those of the bridal party, though they may do so if they wish. For example, a male guest may wear a cutaway and striped trousers to a formal daytime wedding, but he is certainly not required to rent that costume for the occasion.

Formal daytime weddings. To a midday wedding in church, the guests wear what they would normally choose for a Sunday morning service. To an elaborate midday or afternoon wedding followed by a reception, women wear the dressy costumes they would choose for an important luncheon or tea and men wear dark street suits.

Formal evening weddings. If the groom is wearing white tie, a male guest may do so, but he may also wear black tie. If he does not own a dinner suit, he wears a dark street suit. A woman guest chooses a costume suitable for the reception with certain modifications for a church wedding—a jacket or stole over a strapless dress, for example.

PROFESSIONAL HELP—PAID AND UNPAID

As soon as an engagement is announced in the press, there will be many telephone calls and letters from firms offering services of various kinds, some of which you may need or want. However, be prepared to resist high-pressure salesmanship with a firm "No" or "I have already made other arrangements" for persistent solicitors who are offering services incompatible with the kind of wedding you plan. It is always wise to check on the past performance of a firm before making even a tentative commitment, since many are overpriced and unreliable. Good professionals, though, can save you countless hours, and in many cases, can also save you money; their services are well worth investigating.

The Wedding Consultant

If money is no object, the parents of the bride will engage a professional wedding consultant to assume responsibility for all details of a very large wedding and reception. In general, the advantages of such help increase in direct proportion to the number of guests and in the elaborateness of the events.

A distinction should be made here between the very helpful advisers employed by stores to aid and advise clients without charge and the independent wedding consultant who charges a fee for her services. The established professional who works for herself or an agency has managed the details of many social events. She has worked with caterers, florists, and musicians and is knowledgeable about the best ways to coordinate press announcements, invitations, and all wedding details.

For a fee, which may be a substantial one, she will deal with as many of the complicated wedding arrangements as her client cares to delegate. She will get comparative bids from caterers, photographers, florists, and suppliers of other items. She will know where to order a marquee for a garden wedding and will take charge of the food, liquor, decorations, and music for a reception at a club, a hotel, or a home. She will order, address, and mail invitations, write and send in press releases, make sure that the bridesmaids' gowns are delivered on time, and be available to advise and assist in all matters.

Since the consultant is in a position to give or withhold future business, the firms she selects are likely to observe her schedules faithfully and provide excellent service. She usually gets items at wholesale prices and bills clients at retail prices plus a service fee. Since you would pay retail prices in any case, her services may cost less than you might suppose.

You should, of course, have a written understanding specifying the terms of the agreement and the details of the services to be provided.

Bridal Bureaus

Many large department stores provide the services of a bridal consultant without charge. This assistance can be extremely valuable to a career girl whose shopping time is limited, particularly if the store features a "total" bridal service. *Total service* means that a bureau of personal shoppers is prepared to help select and order costumes and accessories for the bride and her attendants; items for the trousseau; furnishings for the new home; presents for the attendants; and invitations and announcements and to set up a gift registry.

A practical procedure is to visit the bridal salons of several stores, make a preliminary survey of the merchandise, and inquire about the range of services available. Select one and then make an appointment with the consultant.

Be frank about your budget. A well-organized bridal department will assemble a choice of wedding gowns within your price range, and also show you various bridesmaids' dresses that go well with them. Very often all these items, as well as shoes, gloves, and other accessories, will be brought to you in a private room so that you will not have to shop in several different departments. The consultant will then order the dresses for the attendants in the color chosen from a sample model, supervise fittings, and make sure that the costumes are delivered at the specified time.

Naturally, a well-paid specialist will not devote many hours to a client who is only doing comparison shopping. But the client who decides to buy the wedding gown, the bridesmaids' costumes, the bride's mother's outfit, the invitations, and part of the trousseau and who will use the store's gift registry for silver, china, and other major items can expect a considerable amount of attention without charge.

Jewelers and Stationers

Jewelers often specialize in fine stationery, handsome china, and crystal as well as table silver, and will be happy to set up a registry of your chosen patterns. They also are prepared to give expert advice about monogramming flat silver and to show samples of engraving on presents to attendants. Their advice about wedding invitations and announcements is especially helpful because they are familiar with the conventional forms and correct wording and spelling.

They also know the rules for the correct marking of personal letter paper and the most popular engraving styles for visiting cards and informals.

When you order your invitations, order some attractive note-paper, marked or unmarked, that can be used for thank-you notes for wedding presents.

Liquor Dealers

Your liquor dealer can tell you the number of drinks per bottle that bottles of hard liquor, champagne, or other wines will yield. He can estimate the number of bottles or cases you will need, depending on the time of day of the reception. Be sure to choose a dealer who is prepared to deliver champagne iced to the proper temperature, especially if you need a considerable amount.

Since it is always better to have a well-stocked bar, make arrangements with the dealer to take back any unopened bottles without charge. This practice is quite usual.

Hotels

If you decide to give your reception at a big hotel, the banquet manager can be exceedingly helpful; he is prepared to give advice without charge about many details of a reception. He will suggest appropriate menus and decorations and give an accurate estimate of their cost, and he can usually supply initialed cocktail napkins, matchbooks, and other souvenirs. He is knowledgeable about the best place to set up the orchestra and the receiving line in the room, and will arrange conveniently located dressing rooms so that the bride and groom may change into their travel clothes. Since he has had experience with suppliers of special services, he can recommend musical units of various sizes, photographers, and florists if he does not have them on his own staff.

Travel Agents

The travel agent offers a number of free services. He makes no charge for consultation. Generally he will make hotel and car reservations and will write up and deliver tickets for transportation without charging a fee for his time.

He has extensive information about passports, visas, and inoculations needed for travel outside of the United States. He can also provide useful tips about climates, clothes, and the advantages of special resorts visited on and off season.

If the travel agent is asked to put together the tickets, hotel reservations, guide services, and side excursions of a trip involving many different stops, he quite properly will charge a service fee. Otherwise, his special knowledge and booking services are offered without charge.

Police

If the principals in a wedding and the guests are such prominent individuals that crowds of sightseers will be attracted to the place of the ceremony, it would be wise to notify the police of the wedding. They will set up lines to keep the entrances free and to prevent onlookers from blocking the sidewalk. They will make no charge for this service.

Musicians

The leader of a dance band is experienced in performing at wedding receptions. He can advise on such matters as the selection of music and the right time for the first dance, the cutting of the cake, the toasts, the tossing of the bouquet, and the departure of the bride and groom.

The staff organist and soloist or cantor are available for consultation about acceptable music to be played before, during, and after a wedding in a house of worship.

See also "Music for the Ceremony and Reception," page 88.

Caterers

Some small catering firms limit their services to preparing and delivering cakes, canapés, tea sandwiches, and a limited choice of hot casseroles. This type of firm may be the perfect choice for a small reception in a residence if no extra staff or equipment is needed.

Large catering firms are equipped to do far more than only provide food and drink. For a wedding in a garden, for example, they can arrange for the extra equipment needed, such as a dance floor covered with a marquee, tables, chairs, coat racks, wine coolers, tablecloths, glasses, china, silver, napkins, and favors. They can provide uniformed waiters, waitresses, barmen, and attendants to park cars.

There is a charge for services, of course, but the know-how of an excellent catering firm may be exceedingly valuable, saving you work and worry.

Unless a friend can recommend a firm, do a little comparison shopping. When you make a choice, insist on a written agreement specifying exactly what items and services are included in the overall estimate of charges. An itemized bill will prevent disconcerting misunderstandings about overtime and forestall oversights at an otherwise wonderful reception, such as no one's remembering to order the wedding cake.

If you plan to use a popular caterer, book his services as soon as possible after reserving the place for the reception. Since caterers are in great demand at certain times of the year, they are often completely booked several months in advance.

Photographers

It is not necessary to have an engagement portrait made unless you plan to send a picture to newspapers with the press announcement. Glossy prints of a recent portrait or graduation portraits can also serve the purpose.

If you are having a portrait for publication made in your

wedding gown, the photograph should be finished about three weeks before your wedding date so that prints can reach the newspapers in sufficient time (see "Timing the Release," p. 30). This formal portrait is often made at the bridal salon of a store after the final fitting of the wedding gown, a practical arrangement if time is short. Some portrait photographers object to working away from their own studios, however, so you must inquire in advance.

If you decide to have a full-length portrait made in addition to the head-and-shoulders pose preferred by newspapers, either the bridal salon or the photographer will be able to supply a satisfactory stand-in bouquet of artificial flowers. But be sure to check this matter when making arrangements.

A portrait of the bride and groom together in their wedding costumes is not made before the wedding day if the standard rules are followed. If desired, this picture is usually made after the ceremony and before the reception.

Candid-camera pictures. Getting satisfactory coverage before and after a wedding is no job for an amateur. If the pictures are important to you, it is better to hire a professional than to accept the offer of a generous friend. In the first place, a friend will have to be too busy snapping shots really to be able to join the festivities as a guest. In the second place, a professional knows how to work efficiently and inconspicuously, a skill that few amateurs have had the chance to master.

Good candid cameramen are in great demand in the peak wedding weeks; therefore, it is wise to secure the services of one as soon as possible after the date of the wedding and reception have been set.

Studios that specialize in weddings have package deals that include the services of one or more candid cameramen and a specified number of candid shots mounted in an album. Compare the work and prices of several studios before making a choice unless a friend knows one to recommend. A good studio is equipped with samples and will be happy to show them.

Standard candid-camera coverage includes the bride's entering the church on her father's arm, the newlywed couple toward the end of the aisle as they finish their recessional march, their exit from the church, the couple in the receiving line at the reception and during the first dances with each other as well as pictures of the parents and attendants, the cutting of the cake, the bride tossing the bouquet, the couple entering the departure car, and pictures of special relatives and guests during the reception.

Most clergymen will not permit the taking of pictures inside a house of worship during the ceremony. There will probably be no objection to flash shots taken from behind the rear pews as the bride and groom finish the recessional, but as a matter of courtesy, the clergyman's permission should be asked.

In some cases, the bridal party reassembles in the chancel after the recessional and poses informally—with the clergyman's prior agreement, of course. This group picture is not posed to resemble any part of the actual ceremony.

Plan with the photographer exactly when and where to have the group wedding picture made and brief the entire group so that everyone will be on hand promptly. Insist that the cameraman complete posing and photographing the group in a specified brief time. Too many receptions get off to a bad start because the guests have to stand around waiting while pictures are being taken.

The group picture of the bridal party and the two sets of parents may be taken on the church grounds, depending on the weather and time of year. Most people choose to have the group picture done as soon as the bridal party and parents arrive at the reception prior to setting up the receiving line. If there is no convenient place for the arriving guests to wait, the shot should probably be taken after the receiving line breaks up.

Expenses. The candid cameraman will shoot many more pictures than are actually needed and will submit proofs so that a selection can be made. He will deliver prints blown up to any size desired, mounted in an album or not, as ordered. The bridal couple usually wants a complete set of the candid shots. Very often the groom's parents want a set for themselves, for which they pay extra. The bride's parents may order extra prints of certain shots and send copies to special guests.

FLOWERS FOR THE CEREMONY AND RECEPTION

The florist should be consulted very soon after the locations of the ceremony and reception have been reserved, especially if elaborate floral decorations are planned. Since the cost of the flowers may be much higher than you anticipate, you may have to revise your budget or amend your decorating ideas. Also, if the wedding is to be in June, September, or very close to Christmas, the services of the florists who specialize in party decorations may be unavailable unless you inquire several months in advance.

Decorations for the Ceremony

If the wedding is in a house of worship, consult the clergyman's office or the altar committee or guild before making definite plans for decorations. In most faiths, there are no restrictions about the use of flowers. They may be massed at the altar, attached to pews along the aisle, banked in recesses and on window ledges, and wreathed around the vestibule. In some faiths, however, there are strict regulations about the placement of flowers, and decorations may be limited to one or two bouquets on the altar or pedestal baskets flanking it.

You must also consider the fact that in certain popular churches, several weddings may be booked for the same day with only an hour and a half clearance between them. This allows very little time for your florist to arrange the flowers and containers before guests start to arrive and to remove decorations before those for the next wedding can be installed. This is a case where the ladies of the altar committee may be of assistance. They may put several families in touch with each other so that the floral decorations for two weddings can be planned jointly and the expenses shared.

If the wedding is at home or in a place other than a house of worship, the choice of floral decorations will be determined by your own taste, ingenuity, and finances. Anything from bouquets from the neighbors' gardens to a grove of exotic flowering trees in tubs are appropriate.

Part of the charm of a home wedding is its intimate atmosphere. This is best preserved by using simple decorations concentrated mainly on the background for the improvised altar, a stairway if there is one, or the door through which the bride will make her entrance.

The choice of flowers is virtually endless. Chrysanthemums, gladiolas, carnations, stock, stephanotis, gardenias, and practically any other type of flower is available the year around in most parts of the country. Modern air freight and refrigeration make even jungle blooms available in midwinter.

Decorations for the Reception

In a reception at home where the rooms will be crowded with guests, low flower arrangements will be lost from view. A few dramatic decorations around windows and doorways, on mantels and chandeliers, or on a staircase railing will be far more effective than smaller bowls of flowers below eye level. You can arrange very effective and inexpensive decorations with a base of greens, such as smilax, rhododendron, feathery spruce, or other evergreen boughs, accented with clusters of blossoms.

In a ballroom or other large reception room at a hotel or club, it is often effective to place tall flower arrangements at the beginning and the end of a receiving line, limiting other decorations to arrangements of flowers on the bride's table or buffet tables—unless, of course, expense is of no importance.

The floral centerpiece on the bride's table should always be low so that she is visible when seated. One of the most practical and charming decorations for the bride's table is her own bouquet flanked by the bridesmaids' bouquets.

Flowers for the Bouquets

The design for the bride's bouquet depends in large measure on the style and fabric of the wedding gown. An old-fashioned round nosegay with flowered streamers has a special charm with a ruffled gown of organdy or dotted swiss. An arrangement of calla lilies is quite dramatic with a satin gown of elegant long lines. A cascade-shaped bouquet is beautiful with any gown and is, in fact, today's most popular form.

Often the bride's bouquet is constructed with an orchid or other single flower placed in the center or on a streamer. She detaches the flower to wear on her going-away costume just before she tosses her bouquet.

A bride's bouquet usually is composed of all-white flowers with green leaves for contrast. Frequently, though, a delicate echo of the color of the bridesmaids' dresses is used in the bridal bouquet. The use of color in her bouquet is a matter of the bride's own taste.

Some brides carry a prayer book in a white slipcover instead of a bouquet, which may have no ornamentation or be decorated with flowers attached to ribbon markers. In the latter case, consult the clergyman if the prayer book is to be handed to him during the service. He may prefer it without flowers.

The bridesmaids' bouquets usually are in delicate colors to match or complement the color of their dresses. Stunning effects can also be achieved with such brilliantly colored blooms as black-eyed Susans, coral gladiolas, and orchids.

Sometimes the bouquets of the honor attendants are slightly larger and more elaborate or of a different color than those of the bridesmaids, but they look best if the structure is the same—cascades, nosegays, or arm bouquets.

The flower girl usually carries a basket filled with flowers. However, she does not scatter the flower petals in the bride's path. This custom is no longer observed, since experience has proved that the routine is too much of a challenge for a young child.

MUSIC FOR THE CEREMONY AND RECEPTION

There is a very wide choice of music that can be played at various appropriate moments during the wedding: while the guests are finding their seats before the ceremony, for the procession, during the wedding service, and for the recessional march. There is still a large selection available even if, as in some churches, the choice is limited by religious regulations to strictly liturgical music.

Perhaps a wedding does not seem official in your family unless "I Love You Truly" and "Oh, Promise Me" are included in the ceremony. Or you may feel the same way about Wagner's "Wedding March" from *Lohengrin* ("Here Comes the Bride") for the procession up the aisle of the bridal party, and Mendelssohn's "Wedding March" from *A Midsummer Night's Dream* for the recessional. Though these are the traditional selections for the entrance and exit music, certain clergymen cannot allow them to be performed in their churches because they are secular, not liturgical music.

If the ceremony is to be in a house of worship, find out about any religious restrictions that may exist. As a matter of practicality as well as one of courtesy, you should arrange a conference with the organist, cantor, or choir master.

If the wedding is held other than in a church or synagogue, you will have a wider range in the choice of music. If it is a religious service however, it is customary to consult the clergyman to get his approval for any unusual musical selection. If the ceremony is performed by a judge or another official, your own taste determines the choice of music.

Music for the Reception

Music is not a requirement at a reception, but any reception is enhanced by background music, even from a record player, provided that it is kept at a decibel level comfortable for conversation. The age of the bride and groom, their musical preferences, the place of the reception, and the number of older people attending will influence the choice of music.

For a small reception at home, records are often the best choice. If you need special equipment, see what local music stores have to offer. Many of them will rent automatic record changers and amplification systems as well as records. For a larger reception without dancing, a single strolling musician—accordionist, violinist, or guitarist—is a popular choice.

If dancing is to take place at a large reception, you may choose any size group from a trio to a ten-piece band. The selections they play are chosen by you and your groom. If there are a number of older people among the guests, it is only considerate to intersperse some sedate dance tunes between the rock selections you may prefer.

If you have set your heart on having a well-known dance band, make one of your first orders of business the signing of their contract. Dance bands are booked for prime dates long in advance.

If you are considering using a talented student band that has not yet attained full professional standing, check out union rules before engaging them to play in a club or hotel. In some establishments the waiters, for example, may not be allowed to work with nonunion musicians.

Have explicit specifications in all contracts you sign about overtime rates and charges for travel time. Union musicians are invariably booked for a certain number of hours starting and ending on the hour—from four to eight, for example, not from four-thirty to eight. If they are requested to stay on for an extra half hour, you can expect to be charged for a full hour extra. This is a customary union regulation throughout the country. There may be exceptions, but make sure of them in a written understanding.

Be sure to ask the booking agent all your questions so that you know what to expect from the musicians—and what they expect from you. Will they need a place to change their clothes? If so, adequate dressing rooms must be available. They will need breaks for rest and refreshment during a long reception. Make sure that the kitchen and bar have orders to supply them with food and drinks. It is a good idea to arrange for a pianist or a trio to stay on duty while the rest of the band takes a break so that there will not be a conspicuous pause in the music at any time during the party.

THE MARRIAGE LICENSE

In every state, a marriage license must be obtained before either a religious or civil wedding can be performed. The license must be handed in advance to the person who conducts the ceremony. Afterwards, he signs it and sends it to the proper local bureau of statistics so that confirmation of the marriage will be a permanent part of local records.

The engaged couple must appear together at a marriage license bureau (located in a city hall or other municipal building) to apply for their license. It will not be issued to one person only.

A marriage license issued in one state is not valid in any other state. Therefore, if you are planning to be married away from your home state, do not assume that the laws will be the same as in your own state. Regulations vary widely from state to state, especially as to legal marriageable ages and to the waiting periods before a license becomes valid. For exact information as to these special restrictions, refer to any standard almanac. They are available in all public libraries. About a month before the marriage date, the groom should telephone the marriage license bureau to inquire about the necessary documents and legal requirements.

Legal Marriageable Ages

In all states except Delaware, Georgia, Michigan, Mississippi, Washington, and North and South Carolina, a man must be twenty-one before he can obtain a marriage license without parental consent. In more than half of the states, a girl over eighteen does not need parental consent, but in others she also must be twenty-one before she can act independently.

In many other states, a marriage license will not be issued to a boy under eighteen or a girl under sixteen even with consent of their parents unless special consent is obtained from the courts.

Waiting Periods

In a few states, a marriage license will be issued on application and is good immediately. But in a large number of states, applicants will have to wait two to five days after applying for a license before it becomes usable.

Required Documents

Virtually every state requires proof that a blood test has been made within a specified few weeks of the date of application for a marriage license. In other states, a general health report is required by law. Do not put these tests off until a few days before the wedding. It often takes a laboratory a week to return a report of a blood test to the doctor. On the other hand, do not apply for the marriage license months in advance of the wedding, since it expires after a limited time. Two to four weeks in advance is a comfortable time to apply in most localities.

Proof of legal age will be required of young couples. If either of you looks younger than your age, take along your birth certificate or other proof of age when you go to apply for the license.

A foreign-born citizen of the United States will be asked to show proof of naturalization.

A citizen of another country will be asked to show proof of identity and citizenship.

In some states, proof of divorce or annulment of a former marriage will be required.

Expenses

The fee for a marriage license varies from three to six dollars. The man pays this fee and the one for his own medical examination. If he and his fiancée go to the same doctor together for their blood tests, he pays their joint bill.

THE BRIDE'S TROUSSEAU

A modern trousseau usually consists of a complete set of clothes that will span one or two seasons, depending on the date of the wedding. A girl marrying in the summer will want a fall and winter wardrobe. The girl marrying in late autumn might concentrate only on her winter wardrobe. In any case fashions change so rapidly and drastically that buying a great deal for the future is not practical.

All items in a trousseau do not have to be new and very seldom are. Most brides base a trousseau on favorite dresses, coats, and suits from their existing wardrobe, augment it with some easily packable dresses for the wedding trip, and add a new going-away outfit and several new negligees, nightgowns, and other lingerie items.

Initials

With the exception of her luggage, which may correctly have the initial of her fiancé's last name added before the wedding, trousseau items should be marked with the engaged girl's maiden initials. Of course, the initial of her married surname can be added later, but items of personal apparel should not be so marked before a wedding day.

Luggage

The bride's luggage is considered part of her trousseau. If she already has attractive luggage, she can simply add the initial of her future husband's last name either following the existing initials on her cases or on the line below them. If she is buying new luggage, she has it marked with the initials of her married name.

If both bride and groom need new luggage, they might consider investing in two complete sets of the same color or of colors that complement each other.

Good luggage is a good investment and will enhance a couple's pleasure in the trips they will be taking together from the honeymoon on.

THE HOUSEHOLD TROUSSEAU

A bride should consider the kind of life that lies immediately ahead of her before she begins to collect her new tableware and linen, since storage space is almost always a problem for a young couple.

The bride moving into spacious quarters, who will be doing a great deal of entertaining, may need at least twelve place settings of flat silver with china and crystal and linen to match.

The bride starting married life in a studio apartment may find that a full set of fine china and crystal will leave her with no shelf room for pots, pans, and everyday table equipment.

It is impossible to list the items that will be suitable to all households. The following suggestions serve as a practical base to be reduced or expanded according to individual circumstances.

Furniture

Many couples find it practical to spend the first few months of married life in a furnished apartment. This arrangement allows them time to search for the right house or apartment at leisure and to choose their furniture without the haste and pressure that so often leads to expensive mistakes.

The necessary pieces of furniture, such as box springs and mattresses and a card table and chairs, can be delivered to most localities within a week or so after purchase. At least six weeks must be allowed for delivery of large and expensive pieces of furniture since orders are generally filled from distant warehouses or factories. Ten weeks' wait may be required if furniture is ordered in a special finish or fabric.

Always choose your first apartment or house before buying the rug, the dining room set, or other major articles. The beautiful, marked-down bedroom set of such royal proportions is no bargain at all if the dresser will block the door to the closet or if there is no room for the night tables.

Silver

Sterling silver flatware has many advantages. It lasts forever. It can be used at breakfast with pottery or at dinner with fine china. It is easy to pack and transport, and it also provides a touch of elegance to a table.

Sterling is expensive, though. Many brides prefer to start with a full set of plated silver or stainless steel and to build a set of sterling by adding a place setting or two gradually.

Whether the tableware is of silver, plate, or steel, the minimum place setting consists of:

dinner knife
dinner fork
lunch fork (also for salad and dessert)

dessert spoon (also for cereal and soup)
butter knife
teaspoon

A service for eight is a good start for most households, and should include:

8 place settings
3 tablespoons or serving spoons
carving knife and fork
4 extra teaspoons for condiments, etc.
butter server

Other useful serving pieces will undoubtedly turn up among wedding presents if the bride lists them in her registry at a store. These pieces may include sauce and gravy ladles, cake and pie servers, pickle forks, and salt and pepper shakers, among others.

If extra serving pieces, or a set of dessert spoons, oyster forks, or teaspoons are heirloom silver, so much the better. A table set with a variety of silver patterns can be charming if the patterns are similar in character.

Initials on silver. It is not customary to mark plated silver flatware. Sterling silver, however, usually is marked with one or three initials.

For example, Mary Beth Forbes who married George Lee Randolph might choose to have her silver marked with one large *R*—the initial of her new surname.

Or she might choose an arrangement of her own initials: *MFR.*

Or she might choose a combination of the initials of both first names and of the surname. When this form is used, the wife's initial is to the left: MRG.

The initials on family silver passed along to a young couple present no problem. Some people like to use the heirloom pieces with initials unchanged. Others prefer to incorporate the initial of their surname into the existing monogram or to have the jeweler remove the old initials and substitute new ones.

China

The most important thing to consider about china is that it is perishable and breakage is inevitable. The disaster is minimized if both the everyday service and the company porcelain is bought at a store that maintains the pattern in open stock. Then not only can chipped or broken pieces be replaced, but the set can also be expanded as the need arises.

A practical set of dishes for everyday use should include:

8 dinner plates
8 dessert plates (also used for salad) *
8 cereal bowls (also used for soup and some desserts)
8 cups and saucers
8 butter plates
1 platter
2 vegetable dishes
sugar bowl and cream pitcher

In addition, a number of supplementary pieces will be needed, but they can be of silver, glass, or other materials as long as they are in character with the china:

1 salad bowl and servers
1 bread basket or tray
4 salt and pepper shakers
1 sauce or gravy boat
1 coffeepot or server
1 teapot
2 jelly or condiment dishes

* Glass plates with matching bowls are an excellent substitute.

trays
6 to 8 tiny dinner-table ashtrays
1 water pitcher

Glass or Crystal

Like porcelain, crystal is awesomely expensive. Since glassware is even more subject to breakage than china, the rule about choosing it from open stock should be observed whether it is crystal or fifteen-cent-store pressed glass. To start with, the new household will need:

8 water goblets
8 all-purpose wine glasses
8 cocktail glasses
8 old-fashioned glasses
8 highball glasses
8 inexpensive tumblers (to be used for milk, juice, or water at informal meals)

Bed Linen

For each bed, the following bed linen is the usual allowance:

6 sheets
6 pillow cases
2 mattress pads
1 summer blanket
1 electric blanket (or wool blankets and a down-filled comforter)
blanket cover
bedspread

Bath Linen

For each bathroom the following bath linen is necessary:

8 bath towels
8 hand towels
6 washcloths
2 bath mats
1 shower curtain
guest towels

Table Linen

Requirements vary widely in the table-linen department. The kind and amount of table linen needed depends on the formality and size of the couple's new home and the amount of entertaining planned. The wife who has a job will probably use handsome paper napkins and plastic place mats for everyday meals and informal entertaining. Fine linen should not be sent to a commercial laundry; very few wives today have the time or inclination to launder napkins and tablecloths for everyday use.

One large damask cloth will be useful for festive occasions: to set up a buffet or to entertain more formally. Eight linen place mats with matching napkins will actually serve very well unless there are several parties each week. In that case, several more sets of mats and napkins will be needed.

Initials on linen. Household linen of all kinds should be marked with the wife's initials: *MJB* (Mary Jones Brown) or *B* (her married surname).

Household linen is never monogrammed with the initials of the husband's given names.

Kitchen Linen

Today, when dishes and glasses washed with detergent dry by themselves without spots, a great many tea towels are not necessary, though some will be needed for drying stainless steel, silver, and a few other items. The indispensable roll of paper towels serves far better than pretty tea towels for drying pots and pans, swabbing counters, and other heavy-duty chores. Sponges, brushes, and scouring pads have replaced dishrags in most kitchens; as a result, today's kitchen linen basically includes only a supply of potholders and tea towels.

Kitchen Equipment

Few people realize how many different items there are in an average well-equipped kitchen, or how expensive it is to collect all of them, especially many of the electric tools. Don't under-estimate the required investment in this department when making up a budget. As a start, consider the following list— and thank the friend who suggests a kitchen shower:

(Note: Extremely thin metal pots and pans are cheap but a very poor investment. Choose heavy cast aluminum, copper or copper and steel or cast iron or heatproof glass or china instead of flimsy thin metal utensils, and don't overlook the benefits of Teflon linings. Buy knives of the very best steel.)

    1 double boiler
    2 stewing pans with lids
    1 Dutch oven
    1 small frying pan (7 inches)
    1 large frying pan with cover (10 or 12 inches)
    1 roasting pan with rack
    2 casseroles with covers
    2 loaf pans (for bread, cake, meat loaf)
    molds for aspics and gelatin desserts
    cake pans
    cookie sheets
    pie pans
    muffin pans
    set of mixing bowls ✓

measuring cup
set of measuring spoons
rolling pin
flour sifter
colander
2 strainers, large and small
grater
food grinder
wire whisk
potato masher
egg beater, electric, if possible *manuel*
metal spatula
rubber spatula
pancake turner
reamer for lemons and oranges
2 chef's chopping knives, large and medium
slicing knife
2 paring knives
wall holder or magnetic rack for knives
sharpening stone
ice-cream scoop
metal cooking spoons, one slotted
wooden cooking spoons
cooking forks
metal pincers
can opener *manuel*
beer-can opener
bottle opener
corkscrew
kitchen scissors
kitchen twine
garlic press
draining rack
toaster
blender, if possible
clock

- coffeepot, electric if possible *manuel*
- chopping board
  canisters
  attachments to hold paper towels and plastic and foil
      wrappings
- garbage can and liners
  kitchen stool and ladder
  bread box
  breadboard
- dish drainer for sink
- cleaning equipment (broom, vacuum cleaner, mop,
      sponges, etc.)

SPECIAL MONEY MATTERS

The importance of consulting a lawyer and an insurance broker before the wedding cannot be emphasized too strongly.

Remember that the legal status and legal responsibilities of both bride and groom are changed automatically when they are married. It is important to understand how this change may, or may not, affect existing contracts and other legal documents held by either of the newlywed pair.

The sensible procedure is to discuss the following matters with qualified professionals who can help you change existing documents or draw up new ones.

Wills

It is astonishing how many people never get around to drawing up a last will and testament.

Don't make the mistake of writing or typing out a homemade will. It is too easy to make some slight error that will distort your true purpose. Consult a lawyer and have him draw up a will that says exactly what you want it to.

Sometimes, an engaged girl sees her family lawyer, and her fiancé consults his own. Otherwise, the engaged couple finds an attorney to serve as their own family lawyer and asks him to draw new wills or amend existing ones.

Insurance

The practical approach to insurance is to examine the policies each of you currently holds to determine how well they will apply to your married status. You will undoubtedly wish to change the name of the beneficiary, and you must decide whether you need any additional insurance. Then get a good general broker. Let him explain the advantages of various kinds of policies. Ask him specifically about:

A *short-term travel floater*. Floater policies cost very little and will cover personal possessions against loss or theft during the honeymoon.

A *personal property policy*. Personal property insurance can be written to cover your wedding presents, furniture, clothes, jewelry, silver, typewriters, cameras, and valuable personal possessions against fire, theft, loss, and other damage.

A *personal liability policy*. Personal liability insurance costs little and is an important safeguard to either an owner or renter of property. It protects against liability for injury to an employee, guest, or stranger who may suffer physical injury while on your property.

Health insurance. Nearly all employed people are covered for health insurance at favorable group rates through their offices. In some cases, additional benefits at low rates are open to married people. Ask at your offices, or call the insurance company for information.

Life insurance. There is a life insurance policy to suit each family's separate needs. The important thing is for a young couple to establish this form of mutual protection as soon as possible. The sooner you start, the lower the premiums will be. Consult parents, friends, and your broker before you make your choice.

Bank Accounts

It is a good idea to set up a joint savings or checking account before the wedding so that presents in the form of checks can be banked. The bride uses her maiden name, of course, until after the marriage, at which time her name can be changed on the account.

Safe-Deposit Box

A box in a bank vault is the safest place to store valuable papers. It may be useful to rent one before leaving on the honeymoon for the safekeeping of jewelry given as wedding presents, stocks, bonds, deeds to property, and other important items of joint ownership. Consult your banker about details.

THE BRIDE'S NEW NAME

With few exceptions, a bride-to-be cannot legally use her new surname until her wedding day. She can notify magazines and book clubs to change the name on her subscription or account in advance, if she likes, but must wait until after her wedding to use her new name on a charge account, voter's registration, and similar documents.

Driver's license. The bride's driver's license, issued in her maiden name, is valid until its date of expiration. Therefore, she can use it on her honeymoon, and apply for a new one under her new name after returning from her wedding trip. She cannot apply for a license under her married name, however, until it is legally hers.

Social security. If the bride is employed, she notifies her local Social Security office (or the company comptroller) of her change of status and name when she returns to work after her honeymoon.

Passports. The bride may not be issued a new passport with her married name until she is legally married. Therefore, if she is leaving on her honeymoon for Europe immediately after her wedding, her passport will identify her with her maiden name. She should go to the American consulate of the first country she visits on her trip abroad and bring her marriage certificate, or her church certificate, to be amended, changing her name. The passport is valid for five years from the date of issuance.

After the Honeymoon

The once-rigid rule that a married woman must never sign her name or be addressed as *Mrs.* when her given name was also used (*Mrs. Mary Green*) has been sharply modified in business, politics, and the professions. The old rules are still strictly observed in *social* life, however, and it is extremely important for the young wife, particularly a working wife, to be aware of both sets of rules so that she can use her new name correctly.

In Social Life

According to the standard rules of etiquette, a married woman never correctly refers to herself, signs her name, or is introduced or addressed as *Mrs. Mary Green* in private life. She is either *Mary Green* or *Mrs. John Green*.

This rule is explicit, and there are no exceptions. It is the first and most important rule that the new bride must learn and apply.

She signs her name *Mary Green* or *Mary Jones Green* on all her mail. If it is necessary to indicate how the reply should be addressed, she adds (*Mrs. John Carter Green*) under her signature.

> Mary Green
> (Mrs. John Carter Green)

She uses the same form when signing any business letter unless she decides to continue using her maiden name at her office. (See "Career Wife" following.)

Her legal signature, which is the name she uses on all legal documents, is never *Mrs. John Green*. It is either *Mary Green, Mary Jones Green,* or *Mary J. Green*.

When telephoning an acquaintance, she identifies herself as *Mary Green.* When making a social telephone call to a stranger, she uses the same form, adding *Mrs. John Green* if further identification is necessary.

When introducing herself in a social situation, at a tea, for example, she may say, "I am Mrs. John Green." That form is more often used by the elderly rather than the young wife, however. Equally correct, less stiff, and generally the better choice is "I am Mary Green. My husband John is on the rules committee with your husband." Or "I am Mary Green—Mrs. John Green." She never says "I am Mrs. Green" to a social equal since that form indicates that she is speaking to someone with whom she does not share a social relationship, for example, an employee.

When speaking to his friends, acquaintances, business associates, and employees, her husband refers to her as *my wife* or *Mary*. He never correctly calls her *Mrs. Green* even if they have never met her. He refers to her as *Mrs. Green* only to domestic employees, waiters, or tradesmen.

His wife observes the same rules. To friends and neighbors, she says *my husband* or *John*. She would use *Mr. Green* only to a tradesman, an employee, or other people who perform services.

The Career Wife

In the business world, the rule for the use of *Mrs.* in combination with a given name and surname is exactly the opposite of the correct social usage. The working wife is properly addressed as *Mrs. Mary Green.* She may be a top executive or a trainee, but whatever her job, she is an individual member of the labor force. Therefore, in her business life she correctly uses her legal name: *Mary Jones Green.*

She should be addressed *Mrs. Mary Green* in a letter, and she signs her mail (Mrs.) Mary Green in order to avoid being addressed as *Miss.*

When making a business telephone call, she may identify herself as *Mary Green* or *Mrs. Green,* or *Mrs. Green of the Blakely Agency,* but she should not refer to herself as *Mrs. Mary Green.*

The career bride sometimes continues to use her maiden name after marriage if changing her last name might be a complicating factor in her business life. This is usually the choice of women who have achieved distinction in business, politics, or a profession as *Miss Mary Jane Jones.*

Wedding Presents

The ideal wedding present is a practical and attractive article that will give pleasure to both newlyweds, provide years of use, and become a family treasure. Obviously, it is difficult to find an item which meets all these specifications. In order to make the selection process easier for relatives and friends, the engaged girl should register a list of desired gifts at one or more stores.

BRIDAL REGISTRIES

One of the better innovations of modern merchandising is the bridal registry maintained by large department stores and by many smaller shops. A friend can choose from the list, confident that the present will please in every detail. The bride is also spared the task of returning or exchanging a great number of unwanted or duplicated items.

From the practical aspect, it is generally best to establish a registry at one but no more than two stores: a department store and a specialty shop that stocks silver, china, and crystal in the bride's chosen patterns.

To accommodate prompt shoppers, the bride should register

her list of items before she mails the invitations. By that time, she and her fiancé will have decided on patterns of silver and china, makes and models of electric tools, colors and sizes of other pieces of household equipment.

A good list includes a number of relatively inexpensive items out of consideration for friends with limited means.

THE CUSTOMARY GIFTS

The receiving of an announcement of a marriage does not obligate one to send a present. The same is true of those who receive formal invitations to only the wedding ceremony. An informal invitation to attend a wedding is a different matter. Anyone invited to a small gathering of intimate friends would most likely want to give the young couple a present.

On the other hand, those invited to a wedding and a reception, or to a reception only, are expected to send a wedding present. Any article, except something for the bride's personal use, such as perfume or lingerie, is suitable: china, silver, linen, lamps, clocks, vases, items for a bar or desk, and so on. When in doubt, a good solution is to select a present from a store in the bride's hometown so that she can exchange it if necessary.

From the Parents

Each set of parents gives the couple a present that will be of use in their life together. The range is wide—from a new home to an old family portrait. A check is often the best solution. Wedding presents from the parents are in addition to personal items they may have given the couple during the engagement.

From the Bride and Groom to Each Other

It is not mandatory for the groom to give his bride a wedding present in addition to the wedding ring, but it is customary for him to give her some special token, usually a piece of jewelry, on their wedding day.

It is not usual for the bride to give her new husband a wedding present, but she certainly may do so.

Wedding Anniversaries

Married couples usually exchange presents on each anniversary of their wedding, and many people like to choose anniversary presents from the following categories of materials. They are associated by long-standing custom with the different years of a marriage.

In some families, close relatives also celebrate the occasion with a gift or a party. As a general rule, special festivities are confined to the anniversaries that are considered the most important: the first, tenth, fifteenth, twenty-fifth, and fiftieth.

FIRST ANNIVERSARY	*Paper or plastic*
SECOND ANNIVERSARY	*Cotton*
THIRD ANNIVERSARY	*Leather*
FOURTH ANNIVERSARY	*Linen or Silk*
FIFTH ANNIVERSARY	*Wood*
SIXTH ANNIVERSARY	*Iron*
SEVENTH ANNIVERSARY	*Copper, brass, or wool*
EIGHTH ANNIVERSARY	*Bronze or electrical appliances*
NINTH ANNIVERSARY	*China or pottery*
TENTH ANNIVERSARY	*Tin or aluminum*
ELEVENTH ANNIVERSARY	*Steel*
TWELFTH ANNIVERSARY	*Linen*
THIRTEENTH ANNIVERSARY	*Lace*
FOURTEENTH ANNIVERSARY	*Ivory or agate*
FIFTEENTH ANNIVERSARY	*Crystal or glass*
TWENTIETH ANNIVERSARY	*Porcelain or china*
TWENTY-FIFTH ANNIVERSARY	*Silver*
THIRTIETH ANNIVERSARY	*Pearls*
THIRTY-FIFTH ANNIVERSARY	*Coral or Jade*

Wedding Presents

FORTIETH ANNIVERSARY	*Rubies or garnets*
FORTY-FIFTH ANNIVERSARY	*Sapphires*
FIFTIETH ANNIVERSARY	*Gold*
FIFTY-FIFTH ANNIVERSARY	*Emeralds or turquoise*
SIXTIETH AND SEVENTY-FIFTH ANNIVERSARIES	*Diamonds or gold*

From the Bride to Her Attendants

Identical presents are chosen for the bridesmaids. The maid and matron of honor may be given the same item, or something slightly different. The flower girl and pages receive from the bride items suitable for their ages. An article of jewelry is always appropriate. Silver compacts and lipstick cases are popular choices. Often the presents are marked with the date and the initials of the bride and groom, though the presents are always from the bride.

These presents are usually given before the wedding day: at a bridesmaids' luncheon, the rehearsal party, or individually at an appropriate time. If it is more convenient for the bride, however, she may distribute the gifts at the wedding reception.

From the Groom to His Attendants

The groom gives identical presents to his ushers. He usually chooses some item of personal use. Cuff links, lighters, wallets, and small silver pocketknives are popular choices; ashtrays, clocks, and items for a bar or desk are also suitable. He generally gives his best man a more elaborate present. If there is a ring bearer, the groom gives him a present also.

The groom's gifts, like those of the bride to her attendants, can be given at any appropriate time; and if hers are marked with the date and the joint initials, so are his.

From the Attendants

Each attendant is expected to send a separate wedding present, addressed to the bride, before the wedding. The gift may be for both the bride and groom. Very often the brides-maids choose to buy one joint present instead of smaller separate ones. The ushers often decide to do the same. The attendants' gifts are usually presented at some special event prior to the wedding: the bridesmaids' luncheon, the bachelor dinner, or the rehearsal party.

DELIVERY OF PRESENTS

Understanding friends who have been informed of the wedding in advance send their presents even before they receive their invitations. Their thoughtfulness enables the bride to get an early start on her thank-you notes. All guests should dispatch a gift as soon as possible after receiving an invitation.

All presents sent before the wedding are addressed to the bride. The enclosed card may include her fiancé in a message such as *Love to you both* or *Happiness to Mary and John.* This rule holds even if the donor is one of the groom's relatives or friends who has not met his fiancée.

Presents should be sent to the bride's residence or that of her parents. They should not be sent to her office unless it is impractical to use her home address.

A present sent after the wedding is addressed to the couple jointly—*Mr. and Mrs. John Carter Green*—and should be sent to their new home. If they are traveling, or if the donor does not know their new address, the present may be sent in care of either the bride's or the groom's parents.

Taking Presents to the Reception

A guest should make every effort to mail or deliver a wedding present rather than take it personally to the reception. It is inconvenient to receive presents at this time, especially if the reception is held away from home. Not infrequently, small gifts handed to the bride at a reception away from home are lost in the excitement preceding departure for the honeymoon. Even at a small reception, there seldom is time to open last-minute presents.

Some presents invariably appear at the reception, however. The best procedure to cope with this is for the bride to thank the donors and to hand the packages unopened to someone assigned to put them in a safe place. This is the only way to avoid the risk of breakage, the loss of the card, or of the gift itself in the confusion of the reception.

MONEY, CHECKS, STOCKS, BONDS, DEEDS

In some families, especially those who still adhere to European traditions, it is the custom to present the bride and groom with checks in white envelopes at the reception. This practice is not in accordance with standard rules of etiquette, but there is no reason not to observe it if it is the established custom in a particular circle. It has its obvious practicalities. Many a bride faced with a score of nonexchangeable, unwanted gifts has envied the girl whose family gave her checks instead.

Usually only relatives in the older generation give checks as wedding presents. A godparent or a family friend whose status is similar to that of an aunt or uncle may also do so. Otherwise, it is considered in better taste to choose some item that can be easily exchanged than to send a check.

A check sent before the wedding may be made out to the bride in her maiden name, *Mary Jones,* or to *Mary Jones and John Green.* A check sent after the wedding is usually made out to *Mary Green and John Green.*

Wedding presents in the form of stocks, bonds, or deeds to property are usually registered: *Mary Jones Green and John Carter Green.* Transfers of stocks and bonds can be ordered through a broker before the wedding but, of course, cannot be cashed until Mary Jones legally becomes Mary Green. Consult your broker for details. More often the donor sends a letter announcing the gift of a specific number of stock shares, a bond in a specified amount, or a certain piece of real estate, and the actual transfer of the property is made after the wedding.

DAMAGED GIFTS

When a present from a local store arrives broken or damaged, the simplest procedure is to return it yourself without mentioning the mishap to the donor. Any reputable store will replace merchandise damaged in transit. When dealing with an out-of-town store, return the damaged present by mail in its original box and ask that a replacement be sent. In this case, too, there is no reason to involve the donor.

If a present wrapped and mailed by the donor was insured, there is no real problem if it arrives broken, unless it was a one-of-a-kind object. Insurance can never cover sentimental value, of course, but it will cover the cost of a present so that you can replace it. Save the wrappings, write a note of thanks, and ask the donor for instructions as to how to file for the insurance.

If an uninsured article arrives broken, let circumstances be your guide. If it is something you don't want, be grateful for the accident, and send thanks without mentioning the damage. If the present is heirloom cut glass and there is more in the collection from which it came, report the breakage to the donor and expect another piece. However, if you know that an uninsured present was bought at some financial sacrifice, it may be kinder not to mention its breakage since the donor will feel obliged to send another gift of equal value.

EXCHANGING PRESENTS

In most cases, a bride should feel free to exchange any wedding present that does not suit her. Mentioning the exchange of a present is a matter for individual decision. If the donor is never going to notice that her electric egg-poacher has been exchanged for a toaster, simply thank her for the poacher and go no further. However, if she will wonder what happened to her present, tell her frankly that it has been exchanged for an item that is giving you great pleasure.

If you return a gift in its original box without delay, most stores will accept it for exchange without asking for a sales slip. If the store refuses, claiming that the item was bought elsewhere, it may be better to forget the matter unless the donor thoughtfully offers to exchange the present herself.

Obviously, a bride of any sensitivity cannot rush to the antique store to exchange a family treasure, no matter how useless it may be to her. She certainly should not sell it, and may even have to keep it available for display whenever the donor comes to visit. The same consideration is due someone who gives you an elaborately hand-worked present you have no use for.

KEEPING A RECORD

Set up a routine for opening your gifts, especially if others are helping you, and follow it faithfully. Save all outer wrappings, as well as the gift box, until you are sure that a card from the donor is enclosed, that the gift is not damaged, and that the gift is not a duplicate or an item to be exchanged. The process of exchange or replacement is made simpler when a present is returned in its original wrappings.

Make a note of the donor's name, the item, and the date

received in a ledger. Even if you expect only two dozen wedding presents, keep an orderly record in a notebook. It allows you to make sure that no thank-you note is overlooked.

If the guest list for the reception is extensive and you expect dozens of presents, an up-to-date record is essential. Without it, you will be hopelessly confused when you face the task of writing your obligatory thank-you letters.

A most useful aid is one of the attractive books designed for recording gifts as a shower present. The pages are ruled into divisions where all pertinent information is noted. A set of gummed stickers is supplied with these gift-register albums for reliable and quick identification: Each sticker is numbered and attached to a present which is then entered under the corresponding number in the ledger.

No.	PRESENT	FROM	SENDER'S ADDRESS	WHERE BOUGHT	REC'D	THANKS SENT
1	Salad bowl with silver base and handles on servers	Mr. and Mrs. William Parks	2 Bell Ave. Lake City, Ohio 12345	Jollifs	Aug. 30	Sept. 1
2	6 demitasse spoons	Aunt Mary and Uncle Bill	850 Fifth Ave. NYC 10021	Tiffany	Aug. 31	Sept. 1

RETURNING PRESENTS

If plans for marriage are canceled, all wedding presents must be returned to their donors. This matter is covered in detail under "The Broken Engagement," p. 17.

GIFTS FOR SECOND MARRIAGES

Friends are not obligated to send a wedding present for the occasion of a remarriage if they sent one for the prior marriage. Close relatives are not affected by this rule, however, and intimate friends are likely to ignore it, obeying the impulse to send some tangible token of their good wishes.

DISPLAYING PRESENTS

Wedding presents are correctly displayed only at home, either at the reception or at a special present-viewing gathering a day or so before the wedding.

The decision about whether to make a formal display of the presents is governed largely by the size of the bride's residence. However, wedding presents are never put on display during a reception at a club, hotel, hall, or in the social rooms of a church or synagogue.

A usual procedure is to clear part of a room and set up the gifts on a series of tables covered in an attractive fashion—white or colored tablecloths or tinted sheets, pastel-colored felt, or any other fabric that will look festive and provide a good background. If the coverings reach the floor, the original boxes for the presents can be hidden under them for efficient repacking.

Usually only one item or unit of a set is displayed: one place setting of an elaborate china service, for example, or one setting of a complete set of water goblets and wine glasses. A pair of matching vases or candlesticks would be shown, though, as would a set of eight tiny individual salt and pepper servers.

It is entirely up to you whether or not to use cards identifying the donor of each displayed item. There are two schools of thought on this subject. One group claims that the use of cards may possibly cause embarrassment to the donor of a very modest gift, as well as to one who has chosen to give a much more valuable present to one bride than to another in the same circle. The other group thinks that a great part of the pleasure is to credit the individual donors with their choices. The cards also forestall the question, "Who sent that?" which sometimes leaves the bride fumbling for the right answer, especially if she has received a great many presents.

If cards are used for presents of checks or stocks, identify the donor but do not specify the amount. If you have decided what to buy with a check, you can add the information *Check from Grandmother for couch.*

The Thank-You Notes

One of the most important social lessons to be learned is that a warm note sent promptly has ten times the value of a letter too long delayed. Therefore, the wise bride-to-be supplies herself with attractive notepaper and makes up her mind to acknowledge as many presents as she possibly can within a day or two of their arrival. It is far easier in the long run to dash off six notes a day during the weeks before the wedding than to depart on the honeymoon knowing that there are scores of letters still to be written.

The rules are explicit about notes of thanks. The bride is required to acknowledge all presents, including those from the groom's relatives and friends whom she does not know. Her notes should be handwritten. The groom may want to send a separate note of thanks to one of his relatives who has been unusually generous or thoughtful, but a letter from him does not excuse his bride from writing her own note.

In all notes, she should express her fiancé's (or new husband's) thanks as well as her own. She also should be specific about the present: *the handsome salad bowl,* for example, never just *your handsome gift.*

She should finish her notes within three weeks after her wedding unless she decides to send acknowledgment cards first. (See "Acknowledgment Cards," p. 121.)

A note to a couple is usually addressed to the wife, in which case additional thanks to her husband should also be made. Or, if it seems more natural and suitable, you may address the note of thanks jointly to a couple.

The best notes are those that sound spontaneous, as if you were speaking to the donor in person. They can be brief—no one expects a long literary letter during the days just before your wedding. What matters is that you return sincere thanks promptly for a gift which represents a sincere wish to give you pleasure.

To a close relative or dear friend, you might write:

Dear Aunt Mary,

Rush—rush—rush, as you can imagine—but nothing is more important than to thank you and Uncle Bill for the marvelous check that came yesterday. I would have written the minute I opened your letter except I wanted to stun John with it last night. He joins me in delighted thanks. Our problem of a living-room rug is solved!

All love,
Mary Jane

Darling Aunt Mary and Uncle Bill,

Thank you so much for the glorious chest of silver. You are so generous. Twelve of everything! I just can't believe it—also can't wait to give a dinner party in your honor. John joins me in thanks, and we both look forward to telling you in person on Friday how very happy you have made us.

A heart full of love,
Mary Jane

Dearest Aunt Matilda,

You are so darling to pass along to me grandmother's cut-glass punch bowl and the big silver ladle. I have always loved them, and John is simply enchanted.

You could not have made a choice that would have given us more pleasure.

Thank you, dear.

> Lots of love,
> Mary Jane

A more formal note to someone you know less well:

Dear Mrs. Johnson,

The very striking Italian tureen arrived in perfect condition. John has not seen it yet, but I know he will love it. It is such a handsome and useful gift. I look forward with especial pleasure to meeting you on the fifteenth because I know how very kind you and Mr. Johnson were to John during his college years.

With very special thanks,

> Sincerely,
> Mary Jane Jones

One present from a group of people is acknowledged in different ways, depending on the circumstances.

If a number of people at your place of employment, or that of your fiancé, have joined in buying one present, it is correct to write one letter of thanks (addressed to the highest-ranking staff member in the group) that can be passed around or posted on a bulletin board. If only a few friends purchased one present together, each person should be sent a separate note of thanks.

A note of thanks to a staff might read:

Dear Milly, Bill, Joyce, Jean, Polly, Grace, George, and Joe (*or* Dear Advertising Department)!

Wedding Presents

Thank you so much for the handsome marble clock. John admires it as much as I do and joins me in thanks to every one of you for your good wishes and for the most unusual and attractive present.

Many, many thanks.

Sincerely yours,
Mary Jane Jones

Acknowledgment Cards

These cards, which do no more than announce the arrival of a present, are only used when you have received so many gifts that you cannot write the thank-you notes within the usual time limits. The use of acknowledgment cards is practical and considerate since many donors would otherwise wonder whether their gifts had been lost in the mail. The acknowledgment card never substitutes for a personal note; it merely gives the bride more time to get through the list.

An acknowledgment card is engraved and mailed in a matching envelope.

Miss Mary Jane Jones
wishes to acknowledge the receipt
of your wedding present
and will write a personal note
of appreciation at an early date

If acknowledgment cards are to be mailed after the wedding, they are engraved with the bride's married name:

Mrs. John Carter Green
wishes to acknowledge the receipt,
etc.

Illustrated Note Cards

Photographers who specialize in wedding pictures can supply attractive illustrated cards for thank-you messages. These cards are social-letter size, and a small picture of the bride and groom in their wedding costumes is attached to it by means of slots or paste. They are not postcards, but are mailed in matching envelopes.

Sometimes *thank you* is printed on this illustrated stationery. This message does not excuse you from adding a complete note of thanks under the printed words. Merely adding your signature under the printed *thank you* is not sufficient or correct.

A drawback of the illustrated notes is that the picture cannot be taken until the wedding day. The only way to avoid a very awkward and conspicuous delay in getting these thank-you notes into the mail is to pick up the cards and envelopes before the wedding, write and address most of your notes and have them ready for mailing as soon as the photos are processed, and then slip the photos into place at the last minute. This means that the bride's mother or someone else will have to look at proofs, select the best shot, attach the pictures when they are delivered, and get them into the mail before the honeymooners return.

RULES FOR GIFT-GIVERS

When in doubt about what to give, consult the bride's mother, her maid of honor, or a friend who can give sound advice about her needs and preferences. Ask for the names of stores where the bride is registered and consult the registry list for ideas. If inquiries are not practical, send a present from a local shop so that it can be exchanged without undue trouble.

Always enclose a card. Your name and address on the outside of the package are not sufficient.

Never sign a card with only one name unless your first name

is so unusual that there cannot be any doubt about your identity. A card inscribed *Love from Ann* will be of no help to a bride with six friends named Ann.

If a gift is sent by a shop, get a receipt so that it can be traced if it is not delivered.

Insure any package you ship. Insure or register a gift of considerable value and ask for a return receipt.

If a note of thanks is not received within four weeks after the wedding, it is reasonable to send a note of inquiry to the bride or her mother. Since the bride should have completed her thank-you notes within three weeks after the wedding, silence indicates that your present may not have arrived and that a tracer should be put on it.

Invitations and Announcements

The bride's parents pay for the invitations, and are responsible for addressing and mailing them. Customarily, they pay for the announcements also. (See p. 173 for exceptions to this rule.)

The invitations are issued in the name of the bride's parents, or under certain circumstances, by some other relative, her guardian, or a godparent, or even by the bride herself. Parents of the bride and groom may issue invitations jointly, but the groom's parents alone never properly issue the wedding invitations except in the case of a foreign bride who has no family in this country.

WHEN FORMAL INVITATIONS ARE APPROPRIATE

Engraved invitations indicate a gathering of more than fifty guests. Otherwise, the invitation should be telephoned or handwritten. Engraved announcements can be sent afterwards to classmates, friends, and the business associates not included in the limited list for the wedding and reception. (Note that announcements are not sent to anyone invited to either the wedding or reception—except, of course, to relatives who would like to have them as souvenirs.)

If all the people invited to the ceremony are also invited to the reception, and the number exceeds fifty, the practical choice is to use a formal invitation to both events engraved on one sheet.

If only a small group of relatives and close friends will attend the ceremony, but a large reception will follow, send engraved invitations to the reception and issue the invitations to the ceremony informally—or enclose an engraved ceremony card (p. 159) in the reception invitations of friends invited to both events.

If many friends and business associates will be invited to the wedding, but the wedding breakfast or other reception will be limited to fewer guests, reverse the above plan: Send formal invitations to the ceremony and informal invitations to the reception, or enclose a reception card in the invitations for those attending both events.

WHEN TO MAIL INVITATIONS AND ANNOUNCEMENTS

Invitations should be received about a month before the wedding, but certainly not less than two weeks before it. Otherwise, people whose presence is especially desired may have made other plans; those guests who want to send a present may feel unduly rushed; and the bride may find herself overwhelmed in the last two or three days before the wedding with unpacking and recording numerous gifts.

Whenever possible, announcements should be addressed, stamped, and ready to be mailed the day after the wedding.

WHEN TO ORDER INVITATIONS AND ANNOUNCEMENTS

Invitations and announcements should be ordered together, since it is easier to address the envelopes for both at the same time.

It is a good idea to place your order with the engraver as soon as positive dates and hours for the wedding and reception are set. In a busy season, he may need up to six weeks to complete the job, and plenty of time should be allowed for addressing, a time-consuming task if you have a long guest list.

Many people do not know that the hand engraving of the plates takes far more time than the imprinting and that, to expedite matters, the order for the engraving can be placed before the exact number of invitations needed is decided. Give the engraver as much leeway as possible. If time is short, have him emboss the return address on the flap of the outer envelope and deliver the inner and outer envelopes before the invitations are finished. The envelopes can then be addressed and ready for stuffing as soon as the invitations are delivered. If the stationer does not offer extra envelopes, order about one extra for each dozen since you will undoubtedly spoil a few.

GUEST LISTS

The final decision as to the number of guests to be invited is made by the bride's family, since the character of the wedding and the expenses of the reception are their responsibility. Therefore, the groom's parents should not exceed the number they have been asked to invite.

Customarily, the groom and his family invite half of the guests to both the ceremony and the reception. The usual procedure is for the bride's mother to consult with the groom's mother, explain the limitations she is setting on her own guest list, and ask for a list from the groom and his parents by a specific date. The groom's family should complete and coordinate their lists promptly, adding full names and addresses so that envelopes may be completed without the addresser's having to check zip codes and other details.

The best way to avoid oversights is for each person concerned to make out a separate list and then let the bride or her mother strike off duplicated names later. Be particularly careful to check the following "must" list.

The "Must" List

The first rule in forming a guest list is that an invitation to anyone who is married must include that person's husband or wife. This rule is followed even if the bride, the groom, and their parents do not know the spouse.

The parents of the bridesmaids and ushers should be invited to the ceremony and to a formal reception.

If the organist and soloist are personal friends, they should receive invitations to the reception.

The clergyman (and his wife if he is married) should always be invited to a formal reception. Do not be surprised if he sends a regret. Clergymen are exceedingly busy men; many conduct several marriages each week, and occasionally, several in one day. Nevertheless, extend him the invitation as a courtesy.

If formal invitations are issued, they should be mailed to all members of the bridal party, and the bride's mother should send two to the groom's parents, with a personal note enclosed, for them to keep as souvenirs.

Wedding invitations, rather than announcements, should also be sent to relatives who live at a distance, and to close friends who cannot possibly accept, as an affectionate way to let them know you sincerely wish that they could attend. Do not enclose reception cards in the wedding invitations used in this fashion except to those who are sure to send a present anyway. Anyone who cannot attend the reception is not obligated to send a wedding present, but the invitation to a reception is sometimes taken as a bid for a gift.

Many people wonder about the propriety of sending invitations to a wedding and reception to a recently bereaved friend. A person in mourning is privileged to turn down one or both invitations, but you should certainly send them so as not to add a small hurt to a big sorrow.

SETTING UP A RECORD-KEEPING SYSTEM

For even a small wedding, a well-planned system for keeping track of invitations and answers will be a substantial help. For a large wedding, a well-organized record system is essential.

The benefits of a good system are enormous. It will give a clear picture of the number of acceptances received and several people can help to keep it up to date efficiently and without confusion. Later, it will be a source for checking addresses for thank-you notes.

A system that is simple and convenient is based on using inexpensive supplies available in any stationery store:

> 3 or 4 small file boxes
> file cards, 3 by 5 inches, to fit the boxes
> 4 to 6 sets of alphabetical dividers
> 4 ball-point pens in different colors

One of the boxes is for invitations, one for acceptances, and one for regrets. The fourth box is for the people who will get announcements. The file cards represent people. The cards can be easily switched from the invitation file to the acceptance or regret box.

The first step is to put the names from the various lists com-
piled by the bride, grocm, and their parents on the file cards.
Place the last name first for easy reference, and spell out the
address as it will be written on the outer envelope.

Albert, Miss Sharon Ann
153 East Sixtieth Street
Lake City, Ohio 12345

Perry, Colonel and Mrs. John Jason
1040 Irvington Boulevard
Chicago, Illinois 12345

If young children are to be included in an invitation, their
names should be added on the inner envelope:

Colonel and Mrs. Perry
    Jean and George

Next, arrange the cards in alphabetical order. This procedure
makes you aware of duplicates, and later will save time in
finding a particular card.

Place the cards for people who will get announcements in
their own box.

Now the master guest list is ready to be divided into three
categories, each with its own set of alphabetical dividers: those
who will be asked to the wedding only; those who will be asked
to the reception only; and those who will be invited to both
events.

As the cards are divided, mark each with an initial. Write
W in one color for those who will get an invitation to the wedding only; R in another color for reception-only invitations;
and WR in a third color to indicate an invitation to both events.
Write the initials in the upper left corner of the file cards. In
the upper right corner, note the number of people included in
the invitation.

Devise another code for those who get at-home cards (see "At-home cards," p. 153) and other enclosures so that any-one—friend or paid social secretary—will have all the information needed for filling the envelopes and addressing them.

As each invitation is completed, mark its corresponding file card with a check.

So far, all the cards are in two boxes. One carries the list of people who will get announcements. The other carries the total guest list, separated in categories by three sets of dividers.

As soon as answers begin to arrive, two more file boxes will be needed for regrets and acceptances. As each answer comes in, switch its corresponding card from the invitation file to the appropriate box. Check each acceptance card for the number of people concerned; if one of a couple accepts and the other cannot come, change the 2 in the upper right corner to 1.

Since an invitation to a wedding only does not require an answer, theoretically all the cards in the acceptance box represent reception guests. A certain number of guests invited to the ceremony only will send an acceptance anyway, but their cards should be left in the original invitation file since the acceptance box is related directly to plans for ordering refreshments for the reception.

PAPER AND ENGRAVING

Just a few years ago, engraving was considered the only correct lettering method for wedding invitations. Now that simulated engraving (raised printing) has been perfected to closely resemble engraving (a very expensive process these days), many brides have decided to economize in this area. To others, a traditional engraved invitation has symbolic importance and is worth the extra cost.

Engraved Wedding Plates

		PRICE PER LINE
SCRIPT	*Mrs. George Fenwick Faulkner*	$5.50
LONDON SCRIPT	*Mrs John Low Venable*	6.00
WINDSOR	Mr. and Mrs. David Wetherell Joyce	5.50
MAYFAIR	Mrs. Percival Harold Clayton	5.50
ST. JAMES	*Mrs. Richard Evans Brooks*	5.50
SHADED ANTIQUE ROMAN	Mr. and Mrs. Lewis Alexander Wilkins	6.00
NORMAN	Mr. and Mrs. Richard Murray Barton	6.50
HAMILTON	*Mr. and Mrs. Oren Chandler*	5.50
SHADED ROMAN	DR. AND MRS. ANDREW JACKSON	7.25

Above is a sample of approved lettering styles for engraved wedding invitations and announcements supplied by Tiffany & Co. to their customers and reproduced here through their kindness.

Lettering

Whether engraved or printed, the lettering must be black, and should not resemble any of the commercial typefaces used for business invitations and announcements.

The most popular lettering styles for either engraved or printed invitations are Script and Antique Roman.

Paper

Choose paper of fine heavy stock for either engraved or printed invitations and announcements. It may be white, pale cream, or ivory, but no other color. Suitable paper comes in different weights. If there are to be enclosures (an At Home card, a Reception card, a Church card, etc.), have the stationer weigh an assembled invitation in its two envelopes. If it weighs an amount that will double the postage, choose a slightly lighter stock.

Sizes

The standard formal invitation measures about 5½ by 7½ inches and is engraved on the first page of a double sheet. This size is folded once to fit its envelopes. Also popular and equally correct is a smaller double sheet, about 4½ by 5¾ inches, that fits into its envelopes without folding.

If the engraved names are short, a raised margin (plate marked) makes a handsome frame. If the lines are long, or if there are many lines, as in a combined wedding and reception invitation, a border should not be used.

Envelopes

Wedding invitations and announcements are enclosed in two envelopes. The flap of the inner one is not gummed.

The return address is embossed in white on the flap of the

outer envelope. It should never be engraved or printed in black. In a less formal invitation, the return address may be handwritten, but printed stickers should never be used. The return address always includes a zip code.

It is of paramount importance to put a return address on all invitations, formal and informal. Too many wedding invitations go astray and end up in the dead-letter office because an address has inadvertently been written incorrectly or because the addressee has moved and the letter can neither be delivered nor returned.

TRADITIONAL WORDING AND SPELLING

Certain rules about phrasing, spelling, spacing, and abbreviations have not varied through the years and should always be observed. A good stationer or jeweler who maintains a department specializing in formal wedding invitations is familiar with the correct details and will not advocate variations. Shops or printers who deal in the raised printing that closely resembles engraving are usually equipped to turn out equally correct invitations.

All names are spelled in full: *Mr. and Mrs. Hugh Stewart Jones,* not *Mr. and Mrs. Hugh S. Jones.* It is better to drop a middle name than to use an initial in place of it. When addressing envelopes to guests, use an initial in place of a middle name only when the name is unknown. A title must always precede a name on the envelope. It is never correct to write simply *John George Grant* or *Amelia Thompson.*

Titles are always spelled out with the exception of the permitted abbreviations: *Mr., Mrs., Dr., Jr., Sr. Lieutenant* and *major,* etc., are not abbreviated except when preceding *colonel* or *general. Brig. general* is also correct if spelling out *brigadier* would crowd a line. When applicable, a Roman numeral is used after a name: II or III, not 2nd or 3rd.

A short house number is spelled in full, but a long one that would crowd a line is given in numerals: *Ten Main Street* and *1910 Main Street* are the correct choices. Abbreviations are not used for *avenue, street, boulevard,* and so on, and the names of numbered streets (unless excessively long) are spelled in full, as are the names of cities and states. Zip codes are not used on the engraved or printed wedding invitation but they are always included on the envelope.

Do not use a comma at the end of a line when addressing the envelope, and use within a line only if the city and state are written on the same line: *Chicago, Illinois 12345.* Punctuation is not used in the invitation either, except when necessary as in *Monday, the third of June.*

Time and date are spelled out on the invitation: *Wednesday, the seventeenth of September.*

The hour is spelled in full: *at five o'clock.* If the wedding is held on the half hour, the conventional wording is *at half after five* (not *at half past five*).

The year is not usually given in the wedding invitation, though it may be. The year always appears on the announcement, and is spelled in full: *One thousand, nine hundred and seventy-two.*

Miss does not appear before the bride's name unless the wedding invitation is issued by someone other than a relative, but *Mr.* or some other title always is used before the groom's name.

The honour of your presence is requested at the ceremony, even if it is not a religious service, but *the pleasure of your company* is the only correct wording for a separate invitation to the reception. Note that although *honour* is the traditional spelling, *honor* is also correct but less often chosen.

R.S.V.P., R.s.v.p., and *The favour* (note spelling) *of a reply is requested* are all correct. *Please reply to* is the usual form when there is more than one address to which an answer might be sent and you wish to specify one—for example, when the reception is to be held at a club and the answer is to be sent to the home of the bride's parents.

R.S.V.P. is never used on an invitation to a wedding in a house of worship unless an invitation to the reception is engraved on the same sheet. However, R.S.V.P. correctly appears on an invitation to a wedding ceremony at a club, hotel, or private residence since it is implied that a reception will follow at the same location.

R.S.V.P. is always used on a separate reception card or invitation.

If an address follows *R.S.V.P.* or *Please reply to*, the zip code is included since it is now as standard a part of every address as is the street number.

ADDRESSING THE ENVELOPES

Envelopes must be addressed by hand in black or blue-black ink. Legible, attractive writing and careful spacing are also important.

The Inner Envelope

A title and last name only are handwritten on the inner envelope. For single people, the inner envelope carries only *Miss Grant* or *Mr. Galt*. If the outer envelope is addressed to a couple, the inner reads *Mr. and Mrs. Bayard*.

The Outer Envelope

Start writing the block of name and address about halfway down the envelope, leaving enough room at the left and bottom for a forwarding address, if one might be needed.

Mr. and Mrs. George M. Bayard
4219 Garden Terrace
Palm Beach Grove
Georgia 12345

Correct placement of the block of writing to allow room for a forwarding address, if needed. Each line may be centered, or any other attractive variant of spacing may be used.

Envelopes are addressed jointly to a married couple, not to the wife only as is correct on an informal letter of invitation.

Avoid the words . . . *and Family,* which indicate that all members of a family living under the same roof are included in the invitation. Not only is the vagueness of . . . *and Family* slightly belittling to the unnamed relatives, it can also cause problems. For one thing, there is no correct form for answering such an invitation. For another, some recipients of such an invitation have taken it to mean "come one, come all," and have turned up with nonresident cousins, aunts, and uncles. If you want to invite the children of friends and do not know the youngsters' names, address the outer envelope to the parents: *Mr. and Mrs. George May Bayard.* Then write on the inner envelope: *Mr. and Mrs. Bayard and Family.*

Young children can be included in an invitation addressed to their parents by adding their names on the inner envelope:

Mr. and Mrs. Bayard
Joy, Roxanne, and Phillip

An aunt, grandfather, or other adult relative living under the Bayard's roof should receive a separate invitation, as should a son over eighteen (some authorities grant young men over fifteen this compliment).

If there are two sons, the outer envelope is addressed: *Messrs. Peter and John Bayard* (or *The Messrs.*). The inner envelope reads: *Messrs. Bayard* (or *The Messrs.*).

Daughters over eighteen may receive a separate invitation or may be included in an invitation to their parents in this fashion:

Outer envelope:

Mr. and Mrs. George May Bayard
Miss Esther Joan Bayard

Inner envelope:

Mr. and Mrs. Bayard
Miss Bayard

Outer envelope:

Mr. and Mrs. George May Bayard
Misses Esther Joan and Peggy Ann Bayard
(or *The Misses*)

Inner envelope:

Mr. and Mrs. Bayard
Misses Bayard
(or *The Misses*)

FILLING THE ENVELOPES

The rules governing placement of the invitation in the inner envelope and it in the outer envelope are explicit and should be observed.

The standard-sized invitation that requires a fold after it is engraved is inserted in the inner envelope, fold facing down.

The tissue inserted by the engraver to prevent smudging of the lettering is not removed.

Enclosure cards are slipped within the fold.

The smaller invitation that fits into the envelope without folding is inserted, fold facing down, with the lettering toward the back of the envelope.

Enclosure cards are put between the invitation and the back of the envelope with the engraved surfaces facing the back also.

The inner envelope is then inserted, bottom first, in the outer envelope, with the writing facing the back of the envelope.

STANDARD FORMS

For Invitation to a Church Wedding

Mr. and Mrs. Hugh Stewart Jones
request the honour of your presence
at the marriage of their daughter
Mary Jane
to
Mr. John Carter Green
Friday, the seventeenth of September
at five o'clock
Community Church
Lake City, Ohio

The invitation above illustrates the shortest standard form for a wedding invitation issued by the parents of a first-time bride. All other formal invitations are based on it. The correct variations to suit special circumstances are given on the following pages. See page 157 for examples of invitations to the ceremony and reception engraved on one sheet.

Note that the year is not usually given, though it may be added after the line stating the hour. If used, it is spelled out: *One thousand, nine hundred and seventy-two.*

The address of the church should be added if it might be confused with another of similar name.

The name of the state is not used after large cities, such as San Francisco, Denver, New Orleans. Although the state need not be added after the name of a town, it usually is to avoid confusion.

For Invitation to a Wedding at a Private Residence, a Club, or a Hotel

The invitation to a wedding at home or in a club or hotel does not specifically mention a reception, since it is assumed that refreshments will be served after the ceremony. Therefore, R.S.V.P. should be included on such an invitation.

If the wedding is to take place at the home of the bride's parents, follow the basic form but substitute the street address for the name of the church. The fact that an address is not given under *R.S.V.P.* indicates that replies are to be sent to the address given in the invitation, that is, to the residence of the bride's parents.

at five o'clock

123 Stone Road

Lake City, Ohio

R.S.V.P.

If the wedding will be at the home of a friend or relative, follow the basic form with this variation:

at five o'clock

at the residence of Mr. and Mrs. Peter Todd Jones

1010 Valley Road

Lake City

Please reply to

123 Stone Road

Lake City, Ohio 12345

For a wedding at a club or hotel, follow the basic form. Give the street address only if confusion might otherwise result.

at five o'clock

The Garden Club

2475 River Boulevard

Westfield, Ohio

Please reply to

123 Stone Road

Lake City, Ohio 12345

For Invitations Issued under Special Circumstances

A widowed parent. If one of the bride's parents is dead, follow the form given below:

> Mrs. Hugh Stewart Jones
> requests the honour of your presence
> at the marriage of her daughter
> etc.
>
> *or*
>
> Mr. Hugh Stewart Jones
> requests the honour of your presence
> at the marriage of his daughter
> etc.

If the bride's mother is widowed and remarried, her husband joins her in issuing the invitation because the use of her name alone would imply that she is a widow for the second time. The words *her daughter* and the use of the bride's last name make all relationships clear.

> Mr. and Mrs. Reginald Barr Smith
> request the honour of your presence
> at the marriage of her daughter
> Mary Jane Jones
> etc.

If the bride's father is widowed and remarried, the explanation given above applies.

> Mr. and Mrs. Hugh Stewart Jones
> request the honour of your presence
> at the marriage of his daughter
> Mary Jane
> etc.

Orphaned bride-to-be. If the bride is an orphan and a relative issues the invitation, the kinship is mentioned. The bride's surname is given unless it is the same as that of a brother or sister issuing the invitation.

Miss Roberta Bethune
requests the honour of your presence
at the marriage of her niece
Mary Jane Jones
etc.

If an unrelated friend issues the invitation of an orphan, the title *Miss* correctly precedes the bride's name.

Mr. and Mrs. George Greer Hall
request the honour of your presence
at the marriage of
Miss Mary Jane Jones
etc.

Separated parents. If parents are legally separated, but their relationship is amicable, they issue the invitations jointly: *Mr. and Mrs. Hugh Stewart Jones.*

If the relationship between legally separated parents is uncomfortable and will not permit joint sponsorship of the wedding, the parent with whom the bride has lived since the separation issues the invitations and sponsors the wedding. When the bride has divided her time equally between her parents, her mother usually gives the wedding.

Divorced parents. If the bride's parents are divorced, it is customary for the bride's mother to issue the invitations, but this depends on individual circumstances. If the bride has made her home with her father, it is correct for him to give the wedding.

A divorced mother, not remarried, follows this form:

Mrs. Bethune Jones
(a combination of her maiden name and
former husband's surname)
requests the honour of your presence
at the marriage of her daughter
Mary Jane
etc.

A divorced mother or father, remarried, joins her husband or his wife in issuing the invitations. Otherwise the implication would be that she is a widow or that he is a widower.

Mr. and Mrs. Reginald Barr Smith
request the honour of your presence
at the marriage of her daughter
Mary Jane Jones
etc.

If divorced parents are not remarried and on amiable terms, they will probably choose to give the wedding jointly.

Mrs. Bethune Jones
and
Mr. Hugh Stewart Jones
etc.

If both parents have remarried and wish to sponsor their daughter's wedding jointly, they choose the following form which explains their marital status. The name of the bride's mother is given first.

Mr. and Mrs. Reginald Barr Smith
and
Mr. and Mrs. Hugh Stewart Jones
etc.

Widowed bride-to-be. In many cases, only a few relatives and close friends are asked to the ceremony when a widow remarries, although there is no reason for the bride not to have a large wedding and reception if she wishes to.

The parents of the young widow issue the invitation in exactly the form used for her first marriage except that her deceased husband's name is added to her maiden name.

> at the marriage of their daughter
> Mary Jones Green
> etc.

For the mature widow, the above form is used if her parents issue the invitations. If a relative sponsors her wedding, the relationship is mentioned. Very often the mature widow prefers to issue the invitations herself. In this case, she uses the name and title that appears on her social calling cards and the following form:

> The honour of your presence
> is requested at the marriage of
> Mrs. John Carter Green
> etc.

Divorced bride-to-be. If the bride is a very young divorcée, she can use exactly the same form applicable to a young widow.

If she is a mature divorcée and chooses to send out her own invitations, the correct form is:

> The honour of your presence
> is requested at the marriage of
> Mrs. Jones Green *
>
> (a combination of her maiden surname
> her former husband's surname)
> etc.

* In formal social usage, a divorcée is never correctly called *Mrs. Mary Jones Green,* and on a formal wedding invitation such as the one above, her name is given as *Mrs. Jones Green.* Today, this form strikes many people as awkward and stilted, especially if the bride is known in business

Invitations and Announcements

Issued by groom's parents. If the invitations are issued by the groom's parents, the word *Miss* is always added before the bride's name, and *Mr.* is omitted before the groom's name. It is not correct, however, for the groom's parents to give the wedding except in very unusual circumstances, for example, if the bride is from a foreign land and has no relatives in this country.

Mr. and Mrs. Leland Grant Bell
request the honour of your presence
at the marriage of
Miss Tania Ortíz
to their son
Herbert Grant Bell
etc.

Professional names. If the bride is known by a name she has chosen to use in her career, and if she wishes to send invitations or announcements to many professional friends who do not know her by her real name, the following form is used:

Mr. and Mrs. Hugh Stewart Jones
request the honour of your presence
at the marriage of their daughter
Mary Jane
(Polly Parsons)
etc.

---

as *Mrs. Mary Jones Green.* It is often simpler, then, for a mature divorcée to have a quiet wedding to which she can issue informal invitations. Otherwise, she may ask a brother or other relative to issue the invitations and announcements so that her name may be engraved as *Mary Jones Green.*

(Sometimes the engraver is instructed to space the lettering so that the professional name may be added after the plate has been used to run off invitations that will be sent to relatives and family friends.)

Professional titles. A professional title, such as *Dr.*, should not be used before the bride's name if the invitation is issued by a relative, but may be used if the bride issues her own invitations.

> The honour of your presence
> is requested at the marriage of
> Dr. Mary Jane Jones
> to
> etc.

Military titles. If the bride is a member of the armed services, she may use her title or not, as she wishes. If she does use it, it follows her name, no matter what her rank.

> Mr. and Mrs. Hugh Stewart Jones
> request the honour of your presence
> at the marriage of their daughter
> Mary Jane
> Captain, Women's Army Corps
> etc.

If the groom is a member of one of the armed services or is on active duty in a reserve force, his military title is used and should be spelled out, never abbreviated.

The title of an officer of the rank of captain or higher in the Army, Air Force, and Marine Corps and of a lieutenant (senior grade) or higher in the Navy and Coast Guard precedes his name.

> Colonel John Carter Green
> United States Marine Corps

The title of a commissioned officer of lower rank is used below his name.

> John Carter Green
> Lieutenant, United States Army
> etc.

Note: First and second lieutenants in the Army, Air Force, and Marine Corps are both written *Lieutenant* (qualifying numbers are not used) in all social connections. But the title of lieutenant, junior grade, in the Navy and Coast Guard is properly given in this fashion:

> John Carter Green
> Lieutenant (jg), United States Navy
> etc.

A noncommissioned officer or an enlisted man may use his rank or rating and his service branch under his name if he likes, or he may use *Mr.* preceding his name in which case he does not mention his military connection.

> John Carter Green
> Sergeant, Medical Corps, United States Army
> *or*
> Mr. John Carter Green

When a high-ranking officer retires from one of the regular armed services, he continues to use his title followed by (*retired*), which should not be abbreviated in a formal invitation.

> Rear Admiral John Carter Green
> United States Navy (retired)
> etc.

An officer in the reserve forces, no matter how high his rank, does not use his title except when on active duty; he therefore does not use it after retirement.

If the bride's father is a member of the armed services and will be out of the country at the time of the wedding, the invitation is worded to explain that fact.

Major (overseas) and Mrs. Hugh Stewart Jones
request the honour of your presence
etc.

Issued by both families. If both families wish to issue an invitation, the imprinting is on the inner fold with the bride's family placed on the left. This form is rarely used in this country, but it is often seen in Europe.

Mr. and Mrs. Hugh Stewart Jones	Mr. and Mrs. Robert Nelson Green
request the honour of your presence	request the honour of your presence
at the marriage of their daughter	at the marriage of their son
Mary Jane	John Carter
to	to
Mr. John Carter Green	Miss Mary Jane Jones
etc.	etc.

Double weddings. If the brides of a double wedding are sisters, the name of the elder is given first on the invitation.

Mr. and Mrs. Hugh Stewart Jones
request the honour of your presence
at the marriage of their daughters
Mary Jane
to
Mr. John Carter Green
and
Joan Denise
to
Mr. Henry Harwood Hill
etc.

If the brides are cousins or friends who are not related, the matter of precedence may be decided in several ways.

If the parents of the brides are about the same age, precedence is decided alphabetically with Mr. and Mrs. Jones being listed before Mr. and Mrs. Parker. However, if Mr. Parker is a high-ranking clergyman, military officer, or government official, the order would be reversed.

If one set of parents is considerably older than the other, they are usually given the first place. If one of the brides' grandparents are sponsoring her, their names would certainly appear first.

Two separate invitations may be imprinted on the inner pages of a double fold, with the invitation of the family granted precedence printed on the left.

The standard form for brides who are not sisters is:

Mr. and Mrs. Hugh Stewart Jones

and

Mr. and Mrs. Stephen Potter Parker

request the honour of your presence

at the marriage of their daughters

Mary Jane Jones

to

Mr. John Carter Green

and

Josephine Mary Parker

to

Mr. Daniel Arthur Simms

etc.

Because of the length of a double-wedding invitation, a separate reception card is generally used. The families should specify where the replies should be sent under the R.S.V.P. request.

Please reply to
123 Stone Road   (or the Parker's home address)
etc.

The envelope should be addressed:

Mr. and Mrs. Hugh Stewart Jones
Mr. and Mrs. Stephen Potter Parker

The reply is worded:

Mr. and Mrs. George May Bayard
accept with pleasure
the kind invitation of
Mr. and Mrs. Jones
and
Mr. and Mrs. Parker
for Friday, the seventeenth of September
at six o'clock

For Enclosures

Any cards enclosed in a wedding invitation are engraved in identical lettering. The paper matches the invitation in color but is of slightly heavier stock. Enclosure cards are slipped within the last fold of the invitation so that they will be pulled from the envelope with it, and not accidentally left in the envelope.

Admittance cards. Admittance cards, measuring about 2½ by 3½ inches, are used only when arrangements have been made to exclude all but invited guests during the ceremony at a church or synagogue. Serving as tickets of admission, they are needed only if the bride, groom, or their relatives and friends are such prominent individuals that the wedding might possibly attract a crowd or if the house of worship, itself, is visited by tourists.

The standard form for this enclosure is:

Please present this card
at Community Church
Friday, the seventeenth of September

(Note that the hour of the service is not specified.)

Reserved-section cards. Enclosing reserved-section cards is a good way to reserve choice seats for members of the two families, godparents, and close friends or distinguished guests. You can do this by enclosing a special card which will indicate to an usher that the guest is to be escorted to a seat in the reserved section. Such cards are often enclosed with an invitation; they may be delivered later in person or by mail.

If an admittance card is issued, the bride's mother may write *Within the Ribbons* on it in black ink. This confusing phrase actually designates the reserved section in front of the ribbons that are looped across to separate this section from the rest of the congregation.

Usually, however, the bride's mother uses her visiting card for this purpose and writes on it *Within the Ribbons* or *Bride's Reserved Section* or *Groom's Reserved Section*.

Reserved-seat cards. Pew cards, which reserve a seat in a specific row, are useful only at an extremely large wedding when it is important to ensure choice positions for especially distinguished guests. They are not often used today, even for big weddings, because hurt feelings usually result when guests of equal prominence find that they are not all placed in seats affording good views. Instead, cards reserving a seat in a special section are generally used. (See above.)

Pew cards are usually not enclosed in invitations except in those to grandparents and other guests who will definitely attend. Otherwise, a card reserving a seat in a specific pew is mailed to the guest after he has sent an acceptance of the invitation.

An admittance card can serve as a pew card if a handwritten line giving the pew number is added. Or the bride's mother may use her engraved calling card as a pew card by writing *Pew Number 6* in the lower left corner.

At-home cards. At-home cards, measuring 3 by 4 inches, are not obligatory, but they serve such a useful purpose that they are worth the extra cost. If the at-home card is enclosed in either the wedding invitation or a separate reception invitation, no name is given, since the cards will be received before the bride is entitled to use her new name.

At home
after the fifteenth of November
5207 Pacific Drive
River City, Oregon 12345

The form above is also correct for an enclosure sent with an announcement. Since announcements are mailed after the wedding, the following form is also correct at that time.

Mr. and Mrs. John Carter Green
after the fifteenth of November
5207 Pacific Drive
River City, Oregon 12345

At-home cards are not enclosed in either invitations or announcements sent to business friends; their purpose is to let relatives and social friends know where the couple may be reached at home after their return from the honeymoon.

A zip number is always used. *Avenue, street, drive,* and so on are spelled out, as well as the name of the state and the date and month.

Train and plane cards. A train or plane card is enclosed in an invitation only under special circumstances.

If a wedding is to be held in the country, and if a great many guests will be arriving from a nearby city by train, a card giving schedules can be very useful. These cards measure about 4½ by 3 inches. They may be engraved, but more often they are printed in raised type on stock to match the invitations.

If guests are expected to take a regularly scheduled train and pay their own fares, the card reads:

Train leaves Central Station at 12:30 P.M.
and arrives at Westbrook at 1:15 P.M.
Train leaves Westbrook at 5 P.M.
and arrives at Central Station at 5:45 P.M.
Express train leaves Westbrook at 5:45 P.M.
and arrives at Central Station at 6:15 P.M.

If reserved space is provided, at the host's expense, in a special section, the card reads:

A special train will leave
Central Station
at three o'clock in the afternoon
It will leave Westbrook
at half after nine in the evening
and return to Central Station
at ten o'clock
Please present this card to the conductor

A plane card follows the same format. A plane card is not used unless the host has chartered a plane or has reserved a section on a scheduled flight at his own expense.

Response cards. For an extremely large reception it can be very helpful to enclose response cards in your invitations. These cards have blank spaces for the guest to fill out which allow him to indicate his acceptance or regret.

Traditionalists disapprove of them, regarding them as correct only for business events or social fund-raising parties. However, response cards are being enclosed more frequently each year because, unfortunately, many guests simply ignore an R.S.V.P. or delay sending the required answer which leaves the hostess uncertain about her final order for refreshments and services.

To avoid this problem, many families decide to break with tradition and use response cards. This is another of the standard rules of etiquette that is being modified by the demands of practicality.

M_____. . . . .
_____accepts
_____regrets

> Saturday, January fifth
> Bristol Hotel
> Abingdon

Map cards. If a wedding is to be held in a house in the country, or if the ceremony will be performed in a suburban church and the reception is held at a residence or club some miles away, guests arriving by car may need a map or detailed printed directions.

Enclosures giving this information may be printed on cards that match the paper chosen for the invitation.

If guests arriving by car will have no trouble locating the church, an enclosed map is not necessary. But if the place of the reception is difficult to find, you can give the guests printed or mimeographed directions for reaching the reception after the wedding.

Reception cards. If fewer guests will be invited to the reception than to the ceremony, a reception card is slipped into the wedding invitation sent to guests expected at both events.

A reception card measures about 3 by 4 inches and is of slightly heavier stock than the invitation, but it otherwise is matching in color and style of engraving.

Names may be repeated or not. The three standard forms are:

> The pleasure of your company
> is requested at a reception
> following the ceremony
> The River Club
> 30 West River Drive

R.S.V.P.
123 Stone Road
Lake City, Ohio 12345

or

156

Reception
immediately following the ceremony
The Plaza Hotel

R.S.V.P.
123 Stone Road
Lake City, Ohio 12345

or

Mr. and Mrs. Hugh Stewart Jones
request the pleasure of your company
Friday, the seventeenth of September
at six o'clock
R.S.V.P.   123 Stone Road

For Formal Reception Invitations

If invitations are issued to a wedding to be held in a private residence, at a club, or at a hotel, there is no mention of the reception, since it is understood that all the guests are expected to stay for refreshments after the ceremony. Examples of such invitations are to be found on page 141.

Wedding and reception invitation combined. If all the guests invited to a ceremony in a house of worship are expected to attend the reception, the invitations are combined.

Mr. and Mrs. Hugh Stewart Jones
request the honour of your presence
at the marriage of their daughter
Mary Jane
to
Mr. John Carter Green
Friday, the seventeenth of September
at five o'clock
Community Church
and afterward at the reception
123 Stone Road
R.S.V.P.   Lake City, Ohio

Note that if the reception is held elsewhere than in the residence of the bride's parents, the address to which the reply should be sent is given in full following *R.S.V.P.*

Community Church
and afterward at the reception
Town and Country Club
Lake City, Ohio

R.S.V.P.

123 Stone Road

Lake City, Ohio 12345

Separate reception invitation. When very few people are invited to the ceremony and a large number are invited to the reception, invitations to the ceremony are issued in an informal fashion and the reception invitations are engraved. The style follows that of a formal wedding invitation except that *the pleasure of your company,* not *the honour of your presence,* is the correct wording.

Mr. and Mrs. Hugh Stewart Jones
request the pleasure of your company
at the wedding reception
of their daughter
Mary Jane
and   (note *and*)
Mr. John Carter Green
Friday, the seventeenth of September
at six o'clock
The Garden Club
Lake City

R.S.V.P.

123 Stone Road

Lake City, Ohio 12345

158

Ceremony cards. Ceremony cards serve the same purpose as reception cards in the opposite situation. If many more people are invited to the reception than to the wedding, a ceremony card is enclosed with the reception invitations only for the guests who will also attend the wedding.

Mr. and Mrs. Hugh Stewart Jones
request the honour of your presence
at the marriage ceremony
at five o'clock
Community Church

The address of the church is added if it is not a well-known one.

For Delayed-Reception Invitations

There are several reasons for holding a reception a few weeks or even months after a wedding. The couple may have eloped, or they may have been married elsewhere and just returned to

In honor of
Mary and John Green
Cocktails – 4 to 7
December 15

Mr. and Mrs. Hugh Stewart Jones

34 Fir Place

R.S.V.P.

their own community. Since this party is not, technically, a wedding reception, the word *wedding* is not used in the invitation. The party may be given by either the bride's parents or the groom's parents, or the two families may give it jointly.

An informal invitation may be in the form of a personal note from the hostess or an engraved informal with handwritten details.

A formal invitation may follow one of the several forms which follow. It should be engraved on standard-sized invitation cards that fit an envelope measuring about 6 by 4½ inches.

In honour of
Mr. and Mrs. John Carter Green
Mr. and Mrs. Hugh Stewart Jones
request the pleasure of your company
Saturday, the fifteenth of December
four to seven o'clock

R.S.V.P.   The Garden Club
123 Stone Road
Lake City, Ohio 12345

Invitation issued by both families:

In honour of
Mr. and Mrs. John Carter Green
Mr. and Mrs. Hugh Stewart Jones
Mr. and Mrs. Robert Nelson Green
request the pleasure of your company
Saturday, the fifteenth of December
four to seven o'clock
The Garden Club

Please reply to
Mrs. Jones *
123 Stone Road
Lake City, Ohio 12345

* *Mrs. Green* and her address may be given if it is more convenient for her to receive all answers.

For Replies to Invitations

A formal invitation to a wedding in a house of worship does not require an answer unless a reception card is enclosed; this does not mean, however, that an answer is never expected. Very often, wedding invitations are sent to out-of-town friends who cannot possibly attend. In such cases, it would be absurd for a friend not to write a personal note to the bride, the groom, or one of their parents, depending on which member of the family he is closest to. Since this note is entirely personal, it is not governed by any special rules.

If the wedding is to be held in a private residence, a hall, a club, or a hotel, an answer is required even if a reception is not specifically mentioned; it is taken for granted that refreshments will be served after the ceremony.

An invitation to any reception requires an answer, as does any invitation bearing *R.S.V.P.* or its equivalent.

An informal invitation to either the wedding, the reception, or both requires an answer. It may be given in any informal fashion—by telephone, telegram, or personal note—but it is generally answered in the form in which it was sent.

Formal replies. A formal reply to a formal invitation is governed by exact rules.

It should be handwritten on the outside of a double fold of one's personal stationery (carrying an address only) or on plain white paper of standard social-letter size: about 6 by 4½ inches. The lines should be evenly spaced and centered so that the answer closely resembles the invitation in general format.

A title always precedes the name of the writer, whose name is spelled in full: *Miss Araminta Lee Perkins, Mr. George Galt Groves, Colonel and Mrs. William Park Pell*, etc.

The reply envelope is addressed to the person or persons who issue the invitation: *Mr. and Mrs. Hugh Stewart Jones*, for example, if the invitation is issued by a couple (not to the wife alone as is correct on an informal answer).

Names should be spelled in full exactly as they appear on the invitation. Abbreviations are not used for cities, states, or street names.

Acceptances. The form of an acceptance follows that of the invitation.

To a joint invitation to wedding and reception, follow the form given below:

> Mr. and Mrs. John Jason Perry
> accept with pleasure
> the kind invitation of
> Mr. and Mrs. Jones
> to the marriage of their daughter
> Mary Jane
> to
> Mr. John Carter Green
> Friday, the seventeenth of September
> at five o'clock
> Community Church
> and afterward at
> The Plaza Hotel

A variant of the wording above is:

> accept with pleasure
> Mr. and Mrs. Jones's
> kind invitation

To a reception:

> Mr. and Mrs. John Jason Perry
> accept with pleasure
> the kind invitation of
> Mr. and Mrs. Jones
> for Friday, the seventeenth of September
> at six o'clock
> The Plaza Hotel

Although it is usual to repeat the place on an acceptance, the following shorter form is also correct.

Mr. and Mrs. John Jason Perry
accept with pleasure
the kind invitation of
Mr. and Mrs. Jones
for Friday, the seventeenth of September
at six o'clock

Regrets. The hour and place are not repeated in a regret. An explanation of the refusal is not an absolute requirement, but it is customary, and certainly more cordial, to give a reason for refusing.

Mr. and Mrs. John Jason Perry
regret   (or *regret exceedingly*)
that a previous engagement
prevents their acceptance
of the kind invitation of
Mr. and Mrs. Jones
for Friday, the seventeenth of September

It is entirely correct for one member of a married couple to accept an invitation to a wedding reception and for the other to decline.

Mrs. John Jason Perry   (or *Mr.*)
accepts with pleasure
Mr. and Mrs. Jones's
kind invitation for
Saturday, the seventeenth of September
but regrets that
because of illness
(or *absence from the city*)
Mr. Perry   (or *Mrs.*)
will be unable to attend

For Informal Invitations

If fewer than fifty guests are invited to a wedding or reception or both, engraved invitations are not appropriate. An engraved formal invitation indicates a larger gathering and possibly a more formal event. Instead, invitations to a relatively small wedding and reception are issued by handwritten notes, by telephone, or by telegram if time is very short. An invitation on an engraved informal is not practical. There is too much information to be accommodated attractively on one of these small notes. A short reply may be written on an informal, however.

Informal invitations are issued by the bride's mother. If, for any reason, she cannot get through the entire list herself, the person who helps always issues the invitation in the bride's mother's name. For example, if the bride's aunt or sister is writing or telephoning an invitation, she prefaces the message by saying, "I am calling for my sister Grace" (or "Mrs. Hugh Jones") or "Mother wants me to tell you that Mary Jane's wedding date is set. . . ."

The most affectionate and natural way to invite close relatives who live nearby is by telephone. However, when time allows, a handwritten note should be sent to them as well.

The writer does not have to observe the explicit rules about spelling that govern an engraved invitation, but may use the abbreviations and numerals common in everyday correspondence.

R.S.V.P. is usually not included on a handwritten invitation. It is taken for granted that anyone receiving an invitation in this form will reply promptly.

The note is addressed to the wife when the invitation is to a married couple, not to the husband and wife jointly as it is for a formal invitation.

Invitation to a close relative or friend:

Dear Janet,

Mary Jane and John (or *John Green* if Janet might not know which *John*) are to be married at five o'clock on Friday, September 17, at the Community Church, and there will be a reception afterward at our house.

Hugh and I hope very much that you and George and the twins will be with us at the wedding and will join us after to toast the newlyweds.

Love,
Grace

In the note above, the address of the writer and of the church would be added for anyone who might need them.

Invitation to an acquaintance or stranger:

Dear Mrs. Patterson,

My daughter Mary Jane is to be married to John Carter Green on Friday, September 17, at five o'clock at the Community Church at Fifth and Main streets.

Her father and I hope that you and Mr. Patterson can come to the wedding and to a reception after the ceremony at our house, which is only two blocks from the church.

We look forward with so much pleasure to having you with us on this happy day because we know how devoted the Greens and John are to you both.

Sincerely yours,
Grace Jones

Mrs. Hugh Stewart Jones
123 Stone Road
Lake City, Ohio 12345

For Informal Replies

An informal invitation to a wedding, even if there is to be no reception, always requires an answer. The style of the invitation indicates that only the closest friends are invited. To be included in this company is a compliment and deserves the courtesy of an answer.

The reason for sending regrets may or may not be given when replying to a formal invitation. A reason is positively required, however, when refusing an informal invitation. It is understandable that when a family cares enough about you to invite you to a small intimate wedding, they expect that you will be considerate enough to give them a good reason for refusing their invitation.

A guest may answer in the same way the invitation is given. When time allows, a handwritten note is the best choice for replying to a telegram or a telephoned message. If an invitation is sent to a married couple, the wife answers.

An answer to an informal is always written and addressed to the mother of the bride, not to *Mr. and Mrs. Hugh Stewart Jones,* as a formal reply would be.

An informal reply should be handwritten on personal stationery, never typed or written on a business letterhead, or an engraved informal may be used for a very short message. The tone of the answer depends on how well the writer knows the mother of the bride.

Acceptance from a relative or friend. The acceptance reply from a relative or friend may be brief. The important thing is to reply promptly.

Dear Grace,

Wonderful news about Mary Jane and John! Give them our love. Charles and I will certainly be at the

church at five on September 17, and later at the reception.

Devotedly,
Harriet

A telegram or answer on an informal might say:

We wouldn't miss the wedding for the world. See you
September 17.

Love,
Harriet
(*Harriet Graves* if there
could be any possible
doubt as to her identity
in a wired message.)

Acceptance from an acquaintance or stranger. An example of
an acceptance from an acquaintance or stranger is given below:

Dear Mrs. Jones,

    Thank you so much for your invitation to the wedding
of your daughter and John Green. My husband and I
are very happy to accept, and look forward to being
with you at the ceremony and the reception on September 17.

All very best,
Jane Peterson
(Mrs. Ronald Peterson)

Regret from a relative or friend. The regret from a relative or
friend might read as follows:

Dear Grace,

    We are so very sorry that we will miss Mary Jane's
wedding to John, but we won't be back from Mexico

until the end of the month. We'll raise a toast to them on the seventeenth—and to you and Hugh also.

Love to all,
Harriet

Regret from an acquaintance or stranger. A sample regret from an acquaintance or stranger is given below:

Dear Mrs. Jones,

My husband and I are so very sorry that we cannot accept your invitation for September 17, but since that is the weekend of his sales' convention, we shall be in San Diego.

We shall be thinking of the young people with all best wishes for their happiness.

Yours faithfully,
Jane Peterson
(Mrs. Roger Peterson)

For Recalling Invitations

If the wedding date is changed, if the marriage is canceled, or if invitations must be recalled because of illness or death, guests who have received invitations must be notified immediately.

Close relatives and all attendants should be notified of the changed plans by telephone or telegram or, if there is time, by personal note.

If time is very short, all guests are notified by telephone or telegram. If time allows, handwritten notes or formally phrased printed announcements are put into the mail as quickly as possible.

By telephone. If the bride's mother finds it unsuitable to make the notification calls herself (in the case of a death in her immediate family, for example) or impractical because of the length of the guest list, she asks a relative or close friend to help her make the calls. The person helping makes it clear that she is relaying a message from the bride's mother with an explanation such as: "This is Amelia Grant, a friend of Mrs. Hugh Jones's. She has asked me to tell you that because of the death of her mother, invitations to Mary Jane's wedding must be recalled. The wedding will take place as scheduled, but only the immediate families will attend."

If the wedding has been called off, the fact is stated without explanation: ". . . has asked me to tell you that Mary Jane's wedding will not take place." In this case, the only correct answer is some variant of "Thank you for giving me the message." If the person asks what happened, the caller should be prepared with some tactful evasion such as, "I don't know the details. I've just been asked to get word to you as quickly as possible."

By telegram. Wires to relatives and close friends are worded informally: *Have had to change date of Mary Jane's wedding to Friday, October twenty-two, same time and place. Love. . . .*" The wire is signed by the bride's mother: *Grace, Grace Jones,* or *Aunt Grace,* whatever is most suitable. An explanation may be given but is not necessary.

Telegrams to acquaintances or to strangers invited at the request of the groom's parents follow a formal pattern. *Mr. and Mrs. Hugh Stewart Jones announce that the marriage of their daughter Mary Jane to Mr. John Carter Green has been postponed to. . . .* There is no signature, of course. *R.S.V.P.* is added if the original invitation included one to the reception. A formal telegram is addressed to a married couple as was the invitation: *Mr. and Mrs. Maitland Lee Fellows.*

By mail. If invitations were issued informally, notice of changed plans is given in the same fashion. If formal engraved invitations were sent, the standard procedure is to order formal announcements of the changed plans. Since there seldom is time for engraving, the messages may be printed; raised lettering that resembles the engraving of the original invitation should be chosen. Heavy paper also resembling that of the invitation is used. The message may be printed on the front of a double fold, but it is equally correct to use a card of slightly heavier stock than the envelope. In either case, there is no inner envelope.

Standard forms for various circumstances are given below.

Circumstances for recalling invitations. If the date is changed, the announcement follows the original invitation closely. No explanation for the change of date is given. If the invitation was to the wedding only, the form below is followed without *R.S.V.P.* If the invitation included an additional card for the reception, the inclusion of *R.S.V.P.* and the address on the new announcement indicate that the reception will be held at the hour and place stated in the invitation but on the changed date.

Mr. and Mrs. Hugh Stewart Jones
announce that the marriage of their daughter
Mary Jane
to
Mr. John Carter Green
has been postponed from
Friday, the seventeenth of September
until
Friday, the twenty-second of October
at five o'clock
Community Church
Lake City, Ohio

R.S.V.P.

123 Stone Road

Lake City, Ohio 12345

If the engagement is broken after the wedding invitations have been mailed, the following brief statement is the correct form for canceling a wedding.

Mr. and Mrs. Hugh Stewart Jones
announce that the marriage of their daughter
Mary Jane
to
Mr. John Carter Green
will not take place

If invitations are recalled because of illness or death, it is customary to give an explanation. The form below is used when a wedding is postponed but no new date is set.

Mr. and Mrs. Hugh Stewart Jones
regret that owing to the illness of their daughter
Mary Jane
they are obliged to recall invitations to her wedding
to
Mr. John Carter Green

If the wedding is posponed indefinitely because of a death in the family, the form given below should be used.

Mr. and Mrs. Hugh Stewart Jones
regret exceedingly
that they are obliged to recall the
invitation to the marriage of their daughter
Mary Jane
to
Mr. John Carter Green
owing to the recent death
of Mr. Green's father
Mr. Robert Nelson Green

If the wedding will take place as scheduled, it is correct and considerate to inform guests of this by adding some variant of this line:

The ceremony will take place as planned
but in the presence of the immediate families only

The form below is suitable to use if the reception is canceled
but guests are expected to attend a ceremony in church.

Mr. and Mrs. Hugh Stewart Jones
regret that owing to a death in the family
they are obliged to recall the invitations
to the wedding reception of their daughter
(names optional)
on Friday, the seventeenth of September
The marriage ceremony will take place
as originally planned

Replies to recalled invitations. A reply to a recalled invitation
is not required except in the case of a postponed reception. In
that case, an acceptance or regret is expected, just as it was for
the original invitation.

ANNOUNCEMENTS

Formal announcements of a marriage are exceedingly useful as
they allow the family to share the news of a marriage with the
many business associates and more distant friends and acquaintances who cannot be asked to a wedding or reception.
Although sending announcements is not obligatory, many families find that it is convenient and worth the extra expense to
do so.

An announcement may be sent to anyone except those who
have been invited to a wedding or reception. A grandmother
or other close relative who might want an announcement as a
souvenir ought to receive one also, with a personal note enclosed.

Mailing dates. Announcements are usually mailed the day after the wedding or within that week. However, this general rule is flexible; it cannot be observed, for example, when a wedding follows the decision to marry by only a few days or weeks. If the couple has eloped or their marriage has been kept secret for a while, it is entirely correct to send announcements weeks or months after their wedding.

Who issues and pays for announcements. Most often, announcements are issued in the name of the bride's parents or other sponsor, though a mature bride and groom or both sets of parents may issue an announcement jointly.

Usually, the bride's parents pay for the announcements, but if the groom's parents wish to send out a large number, it is correct for them to suggest paying for their share. They do not issue the announcements in their own name, however. The wording in this case remains exactly the same as in the basic form given below unless the parents decide to send out a joint announcement, which has long been the custom in Europe. This is a practical way for the parents of the groom to share the spotlight equally with the parents of the bride. The European style is like that of the wedding invitation issued by both families jointly shown on page 150. The joint announcement form on page 174 is more often used in this country.

Press announcements. Newspaper announcements of both engagements and weddings are dealt with under "Press Announcements," starting on page 29.

Announcement Forms

A formal announcement follows the rules for a formal wedding invitation in size, type of paper and engraving, use of two envelopes, addressing, and other details, with a few differences in wording.

The year is always given as well as the date.

The name of the city or town where the marriage took place is given.

If the wedding was in a house of worship, its name may be added following the year, but this is optional. If the wedding was held elsewhere than in a house of worship, no mention is made of the place.

Basic announcement form. The form for a basic announcement is given below.

Mr. and Mrs. Hugh Stewart Jones
have the honour of announcing *
the marriage of their daughter
Mary Jane
to
Mr. John Carter Green
Friday, the seventeenth of September
One thousand, nine hundred and seventy-two
Lake City, Ohio

* Or *have the honour to announce* or *announce.*

Joint announcement form issued by both families. If both families wish to announce a marriage, they should follow the example given below:

Mr. and Mrs. Hugh Stewart Jones
and
Mr. and Mrs. Robert Nelson Green
have the honour to announce the marriage of
Mary Jane Jones
and
John Carter Green
on
etc.

Joint announcement form issued by the bride and groom. If both the bride and the groom wish to announce their wedding and it is the bride's first marriage, the correct form is:

Miss Mary Jane Jones
and
Mr. John Carter Green
announce their marriage
on
etc.

If the bride is a widow or divorcée, the same rules apply as for her wedding invitations. See that section on page 146 for the various choices.

Replies to an Announcement

An announcement carries no obligation to send a wedding present, and, technically, it does not require an answer. However, if someone has taken the trouble to share this important family news, it is only natural and kind to send a personal note to the bride, groom, or one of the parents.

Special Events—Just Before and Just After the Wedding

Certain festivities occurring prior to the wedding and immediately after the reception have become customary parts of a formal wedding, though they are not obligatory and some people choose to dispense with them.

THE BACHELOR PARTY

The bachelor party is steadily losing popularity. One reason for this is that many grooms find parties that include the bride and bridesmaids more fun than the all-male bachelor dinner.

The stag party at which the groom, best man, ushers, and other friends of the groom gather to mark his farewell to bachelor freedom was once traditionally held on the evening before the wedding. Frequently it resulted in too many conspicuous hangovers on the wedding day. Today, the bachelor party is scheduled several days before the marriage date.

The groom may be the host, the best man may give the party, or the ushers may share the expenses for it.

The only way in which it differs from any other dinner party for men is in giving the traditional toast to the bride. At an appropriate time during the meal, the groom rises, proposes a toast to his wife-to-be, and all present rise and drink to her.

It is not a current custom to drain and then shatter the toasting glasses. If the groom either cracks the stem of his glass between his fingers or hurls it into a fireplace, everyone follows suit; if the groom does not destroy his glass, no one else does either.

If there is a bachelor dinner, the groom usually takes this opportunity to give his best man and ushers their wedding presents as well as his thanks for serving as his attendants.

THE BRIDE'S PARTY FOR HER BRIDESMAIDS

Sometimes the bride decides to have an all-girl supper party for her bridesmaids and other close friends while her fiancé is having his bachelor dinner. More often, the bride gives a luncheon or tea for her bridesmaids during the week before the wedding. Even if the party is held at a restaurant, it often ends at the bride's residence in order for her to display her trousseau and wedding presents.

At some suitable time during the party, the bride gives her attendants the presents she has chosen to thank them for serving in her wedding.

PARTIES FOR OUT-OF-TOWNERS

If a wedding is to be held in the late afternoon, the bride's mother would undoubtedly appreciate one of her friends giving a luncheon for out-of-town relatives. More than likely, she will be far too busy with her own last-minute preparations for the wedding and reception to do more than hope that out-of-town guests are not feeling neglected.

A luncheon for the bridesmaids and ushers might also be very welcome. This would certainly be helpful if the ceremony is to be held in the early evening followed by a reception at which dinner will be served. Depending on the locality and the number of out-of-town attendants, a luncheon party may be the only solution to the problem of filling a long day. Not infrequently, the bride and groom will attend also. The superstition that it is unlucky for the groom to see his bride on their wedding day is generally ignored by today's level-headed young people. In any case, friends who can conveniently do so will be greatly appreciated if they offer to entertain. The bride's mother can always refuse, but very often she will accept gratefully.

PARTIES AFTER THE RECEPTION

Not infrequently, close friends of the parents will plan a dinner for them following an afternoon reception. The bride's parents themselves may give a back-to-the-house party for close relatives if some are from out of town, which may well be their first chance to catch up on family news. Here again, having firm plans will make such a gathering go more smoothly. The bride's mother is well advised not to leave an after-reception meal to chance. She should either plan a dinner with a few relatives and friends or suggest to the visiting friends that they make their own arrangements for the evening.

ATTENDANTS' PARTIES

There is no end to the parties that may be given by members of the bridal party, though obviously too many parties very shortly before the ceremony can be tiring and even deflect a bit of the excitement from the reception. For this reason, most parties given by the attendants are usually held in advance of the bachelor party and the rehearsal dinner, which always occur within two or three days of the wedding.

Parties given by the bridesmaids may follow an event such as the first fitting of the wedding costumes and may be a morning coffee, luncheon, cocktail party, or dinner. The party may honor the bride or it may be for both the bride and groom, in which case the ushers are also invited.

Often the bridesmaids and ushers together decide to sponsor a party for the engaged pair. A dance, barbecue, picnic, or swimming party is a good choice.

Although these parties are not obligatory, they can be a very pleasant part of an engagement.

PRESENT-VIEWING PARTIES

Present-viewing parties are discussed under "Displaying Presents," p. 117.

SHOWERS

To serve their purpose, showers should be held well in advance of the wedding. They are discussed under "Engagements," p. 24.

THE REHEARSAL

There is no need to hold a rehearsal prior to an informal wedding. Instead, the clergyman or a member of his staff will give the principals a short briefing before the ceremony so that they will know in what order to enter, where to stand, and so on. He may talk with the groom and the best man alone and then with the bride, her attendants, and her father if she is to be given away by him. Or he may choose to explain the procedures to all the participants at the same time.

A complete rehearsal is essential for even a relatively small formal wedding, however. If the event is to function smoothly and with the dignity it deserves, the entire proceeding should be rehearsed, from the arrival of the ushers to the departure of the bridal party for the reception. The ushers will need briefing on how to escort a single lady or gentleman, a couple, or a whole family to their seats; how and when to seat the parents of the groom and the mother of the bride; and how to usher them out. They must know when to loop the aisle ribbons and when and how to get signals to the organist, among other responsibilities.

The organist must be present in order for the group to practice the correct slow pace of the procession up the aisle. The spacing between individuals and between groups must be under perfect control. It is also essential that each member of the bridal party know exactly where to stand and what to do before, during, and after the marriage service.

The words of the marriage service are not spoken during the rehearsal, but the clergyman explains each part in detail in order to avoid confusion about such matters as where the bride's father stands, when the maid of honor takes charge of the bride's bouquet and when she returns it, when and by whom the bride's veil is raised, and the order of the recessional. There are many important details that cannot be left to chance, particularly since they can vary considerably in different faiths.

It is no longer customary for the bride to watch the rehearsal while a stand-in substitutes for her. After all, since she is the star of the occasion, the best safeguard against mishaps is for her to practice her own part during the rehearsal.

Wedding clothes are not worn to the rehearsal, of course, but those attending are expected to dress and behave with a degree of formality suitable to the place and occasion.

The rehearsal may be held at any convenient hour, but there is an unwritten rule that it never follows a cocktail party, for obvious reasons. The most popular time is at about five or five-thirty in the afternoon if the usual rehearsal dinner is to follow. This hour usually is the most convenient for the clergyman. Attendants who have jobs may have to leave their offices early in order to arrive on time. If some of the attendants are coming from out of town, the rehearsal may have to be scheduled for the evening before the wedding, but generally it is held a day or two in advance.

Usually only the wedding participants attend the rehearsal, but there is no firm rule guiding this. If grandparents and other close relatives wish to watch, they may certainly do so. If there is to be a rehearsal party, the mates of the married attendants may find it convenient to attend the rehearsal and then go along with the bridal party to the rehearsal dinner. Since everyone will be together at the rehearsal, this is an opportune time to inform them about when and where the group picture of the wedding party will be made after the ceremony.

Items to take to the rehearsal. It is a good idea for the groom to deliver the marriage license to the clergyman or his secretary for safekeeping at this time in order to avoid the possibility of his forgetting or misplacing it on the wedding day.

The rehearsal is also an excellent time for the father of the bride to deliver checks to the organist, soloist, sexton, or other persons connected with the church staff to whom fees are due.

If special mass books have been ordered and delivered to the bride's parents, they can be left in the church office for the wedding day as can the supply of maps or printed directions showing guests how to get to the place of the reception from the church.

Three "stand-in" bouquets will be needed by the bride and

two of her attendants for practice. They can be made from ruffles of tissue paper or loops of the ribbons collected from wedding presents.

Be sure to bring along typed lists of names of guests to be seated in the reserved sections with pew numbers as needed. These lists are for the ushers to study. You might also prepare duplicates to be distributed to the ushers on the wedding day.

The Rehearsal Dinner

It is customary for the groom's parents to give the dinner party following the rehearsal, though it is equally correct for the bride's parents to give it.

The event may be an informal backyard buffet of cold cuts and salads or a formal sit-down dinner in the private dining room of a club or hotel.

The rehearsal dinner is likely to be a sizable undertaking. All attendants are always invited; it is also polite to include the wife or husband of a married attendant and to ask the fiancé or fiancée of an engaged attendant. The parents of a ring bearer and flower girl are invited, though they will usually leave these very young attendants with a baby-sitter unless the hostess has made special provision for them. If the clergyman is a family friend or from out of town, he is included as is his wife. Otherwise the clergyman is not invited to this gathering. Special out-of-town relatives may also be invited. If one set of grandparents is asked, the other must be also.

The guest list is discussed by the two mothers, no matter which one is the hostess, before final plans take shape. If the groom's parents are giving the party and if they are coming from some distance for the wedding, the groom's mother may ask the bride's mother to reserve space at a club or hotel. She can then complete arrangements for the menu by mail or long-distance telephone.

Invitations should be sent about two weeks in advance. They may be issued by telephone, but if the list is fairly long, it is more practical to send short personal notes or use informals in this fashion:

Rehearsal Dinner for
Mary Jane & John.

Mr. and Mrs. Robert Nelson Green

Wednesday, Sept 15 – 7 pm.
The Shore Club

R.S.V.P.
150 Klickitat Ave.
Portland, Oregon 12345

This event is a good opportunity for the exchange of toasts, although there is no established protocol concerning them. The bride and groom may use the occasion to give their attendants their wedding presents if they have not done so at a prior gathering.

The prime rules to remember in assigning seats at a rehearsal dinner is that the bride and groom sit together, with the bride always placed on his right. If the groom's parents are the host and hostess, the bride's parents are given the ranking places of honor on their respective right sides. The reverse is the rule if the bride's parents give the party. If the clergyman attends, he should be seated at the left of the hostess. His wife would not take precedence over a grandparent or other special guest, but she may correctly be seated anywhere along the side of the table.

Place cards will obviously be needed if a large group is to be seated at one table.

Rehearsal Dinner—Seating at a Rectangular Table

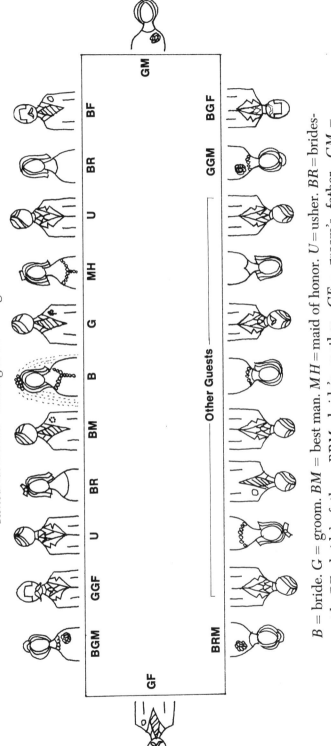

B = bride. G = groom. BM = best man. MH = maid of honor. U = usher. BR = brides-maid. BF = bride's father. BRM = bride's mother. GF = groom's father. GM = groom's mother. BGM = bride's grandmother. BGF = bride's grandfather. GGM = groom's grandmother. GGF = groom's grandfather.

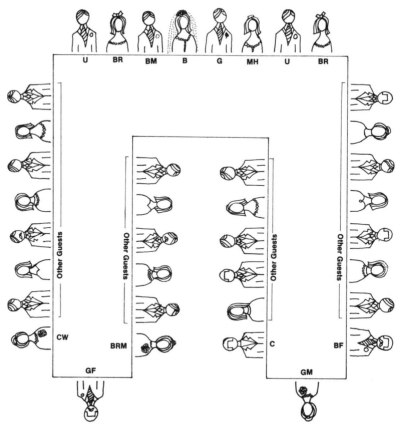

B = bride. G = groom. BM = best man. MH = maid of honor. U = usher. BR = bridesmaid. BF = bride's father. BRM = bride's mother. GF = groom's father. GM = groom's mother. C = clergyman. CW = clergyman's wife.

The Wedding

The first part of this chapter is devoted to the standard procedures for a formal wedding as conducted in all major Protestant denominations, though there may be several details that will change from group to group.

Following it are sections dealing with the differences in the rituals observed in the Protestant Episcopal faith, in the Roman Catholic, Greek Orthodox, and other churches of the Eastern rite; in the Reform, Conservative, and Orthodox Jewish congregations; and in the Quaker, the Mormon, and the Christian Science faiths.

Towards the end of the chapter, the details concerning double weddings, military weddings, marriages conducted by civil authorities, and weddings held in various locations other than a house of worship are given.

It should be remembered that rules and customs within each faith are changing and also that different procedures are permitted in different divisions and areas of the same faith.

Some clergymen are willing to break with tradition within reasonable limits. Others feel that the strict observance of established regulations is important to the meaning of organized religion.

This chapter gives the basic procedures approved in different faiths, but it should be kept in mind that the minister, priest, or rabbi who will officiate has the final word about the possibility of changes.

Standard Seating Plans

In a house of worship with a center aisle, the bride's section is on the left as one faces the altar; the groom's section is on the right.

The parents occupy the first pews, the fathers in the aisle seats. Relatives sit with them and in the pews immediately behind them. If there is a large reserved section, guests seated in it should include godparents; exceptionally close family friends; the wives, husbands, and parents of attendants; teachers to whom the bride and groom are especially devoted; employees who have been very close to them since childhood; and guests who need special consideration because of an infirmity.

Obviously, very large reserved sections can present many problems—anyone who has served on the seating committee of a charity banquet or a fund-raising theater party will certainly realize this. Many parents have discovered that the most tactful solution is to reserve only three or four rows to accommodate the closest relatives. The ushers can then seat all other guests on a first-come-first-served basis; in this way, it is easier to avoid the likelihood of hurt feelings among those who do not receive cards for the reserved section.

If the families live in the same vicinity, the mothers work out plans for the reserved section together, deciding on the division of mutual friends so that there will not be a marked imbalance between the two sides of the aisle. Otherwise, they confer by mail or telephone about their reserved lists, and the bride's mother sends out the cards in one of the forms described on page 153.

There are several ways to seat a church that has a solid

central section flanked by two side sections. The most usual arrangements are shown in the following charts.

BF = bride's father
GF = groom's father
BRM = bride's mother
GM = groom's mother

If relatively few people will be present, the right aisle is treated as if it were a center aisle in all details and the rest of the pews are ignored. The marriage is held at the head of the right aisle.

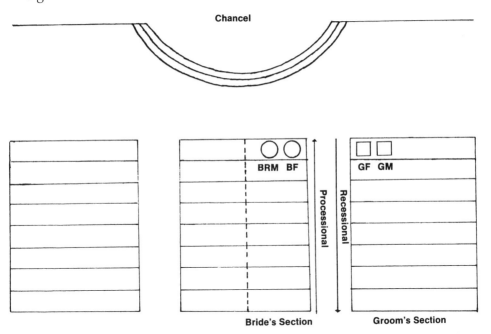

Or all the guests may be seated in the center section. In this case, the procession goes up the left aisle and the recessional is down the right aisle.

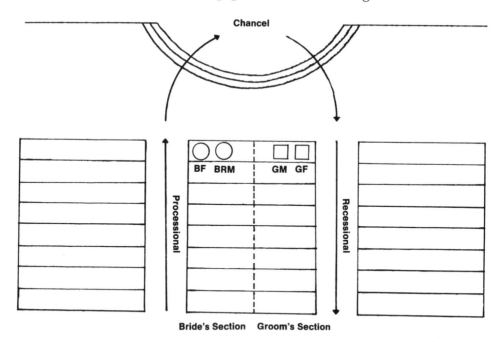

Bride's Section   Groom's Section

If the church will be fully seated, two arrangements are possible. In both, the procession may go up either the right or the left aisle.

Seating Divorced Parents

Divorced parents do not occupy the same pew, according to the rules of etiquette, even if they have remained on amiable terms.

The bride's mother occupies the first pew with her mother and father or other members of her immediate family beside her or in one or two pews immediately behind her. The bride's father, after giving his daughter away, takes his place in the pew behind those occupied by his former in-laws. His own family sits beside and immediately behind him.

If the bride has brothers and sisters who are not serving as attendants, the best position for them is in one of the pews between their father and mother.

If the bride's parents have remarried, her mother sits in the

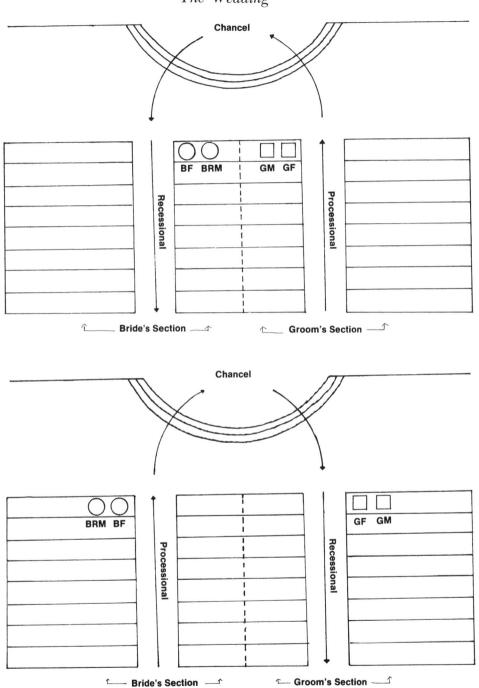

first pew with her current husband beside her, and the bride's relatives on her mother's side sit in the next rows. The bride's father, her stepmother, and their children, if any, occupy the next pew with the bride's paternal grandparents, aunts, and uncles in the succeeding pews. There is no problem if the divorced parents are on good terms with each other.

If there is great bitterness between divorced parents, some kind of compromise must be reached. It is the duty of the bride to make the final decision, which may be a painful, if not impossible, task. It is this kind of family impasse that occasionally can be solved only by an elopement. If the bride does want a wedding, however, and if the parents cannot bring themselves to meet, the father may call for his daughter, escort her up the aisle, give her away, depart after the ceremony, and not attend the reception.

SEATING THE GUESTS

The ushers should arrive at the place of the ceremony an hour before a large wedding, forty-five minutes before a smaller one.

Although their boutonnieres and gloves may be delivered to them elsewhere, generally it is most practical to put their flowers in charge of the sexton and have them waiting at the house of worship.

They review their instructions and the lists of those who are to be shown to the reserved sections, put on their gloves, and wait in the vestibule ready for duty.

Considerate guests, realizing that a rush of last-minute arrivals can delay the start of the ceremony, make a point of being early. All guests should plan to arrive and be in their seats ten minutes before the announced hour. Guests should wait in the vestibule to be escorted to seats; they should not "help" by finding their own places. This often happens where many guests arrive at once and all cannot be seated immediately.

The Wedding

When a guest arrives, an usher steps forward, bows, and greets anyone he knows. Since this is a joyous social occasion, it is perfectly permissible for guests and ushers to exchange small talk as they proceed along the aisle.

It is not customary today for the ushers to ask "Bride's or groom's section?" if the guest does not produce a reserved-seat card or if he does not tell the usher that he is a member of one of the families. It is often awkward for a guest to answer that question if he is friendly with both families. If a guest requests one section, the usher complies, of course. If the groom and his parents are not local residents, so that his side will be very sparsely filled, the ushers volunteer, "We are seating both sides equally," in which case the guest accepts the pew indicated without comment.

When practical, each lady is escorted to her seat on the arm of an usher. If two ladies arrive together and only one usher is available at the moment, he offers his right arm to the elder and the younger follows a few paces behind. When a family group arrives, an usher escorts the wife. Her children and husband follow, usually in pairs.

An usher never offers his left arm to a guest or walks up the aisle between a couple. He never offers his arm to a man unless the gentleman is incapacitated and in need of assistance. Instead, they walk side by side, the male guest on the usher's right.

When there are several ushers and many guests arriving at once, the traffic up the main aisle moves more smoothly if the ushers continue to the head of the main aisle after seating a party, cross to a side aisle, and return by that aisle.

Guests who arrive early are privileged to take the aisle seats if they are shown to an empty pew. They are not expected to move over when others join them in the row. They either rise or turn their knees aside to let the other guests reach inner seats.

ASSEMBLING THE WEDDING PARTY

The groom and the best man arrive together about half an hour before the ceremony. They enter through a side door and wait in the vestry.

There is a fixed order in which the bride's mother, the bridesmaids, the bride, and her father arrive at the place of the wedding. Transportation has to be carefully planned and timed and some arrangement must be made for the bride's party to gather in one place so that it can leave in proper order.

If the bride's home is large enough, it may be most convenient for the bridesmaids to dress there. Many churches are equipped with dressing rooms for just such occasions. If the bridesmaids dress at their own homes, they gather at the bride's residence for a last-minute check of their make-up, headdresses, and costumes and to receive their bouquets.

The bride's mother leaves in the first car, alone or with one of the attendants, depending on the number of cars provided. She should arrive about five minutes before the time announced for the ceremony. She enters through the main door and waits in the vestibule in a place determined at the rehearsal until it is time for her to be escorted to her pew.

The bridesmaids follow in the next cars, usually no more than two together so that their costumes will not be crushed. They enter by a side door and assemble in a secluded part of the vestibule or other space determined at the rehearsal. They stand in the planned order of the procession.

The bride and her father leave in the last car. She sits on her father's right. They enter the side door just a minute or so before the hour of the ceremony and take their places in the processional line-up.

In the meantime, the groom's parents have entered the main door a few minutes before the bride's mother arrives. They wait on the groom's side of the vestibule, where the bride's mother usually joins them for the few minutes before they are seated. Their coats may be sent to their seats in advance.

If the entire wedding party has arrived on schedule, the ushers should be able to close the outer doors as a signal to late-comers that the ceremony is about to begin and that no more guests will be escorted to seats. Guests arriving after this time may slip into places from the side aisles, but should not use the center aisle.

The head usher escorts the mother of the groom to the front pew on the right with the groom's father following a few paces behind.

The mother of the bride is always the last to be escorted to her place. If she has a son who is acting as an usher, he takes her to her seat. If she has two sons, the older seats her and the younger escorts her out after the ceremony.

As soon as the mother of the bride is seated, two ushers advance side by side to the back of the reserved section, turn, and walk to the rear, looping the ribbons that enclose the major portion of the congregation across the ends of the pews.

While the aisle ribbons are being looped in place, two other ushers (or members of the sexton's staff) advance up the side aisles; pick up the aisle canvas, which is in place at the foot of the altar, by its handles; and walk to the rear, stretching its white length smoothly down the main aisle. All the ushers then take their places at the head of the bridal procession.

Most churches have a buzzer system so that signals can be sent to the vestry and the organist to begin. Otherwise, the sexton or someone else delegated for the duty takes the message. The clergyman then enters from the vestry followed by the bridegroom and the best man walking together.

The clergyman takes his place facing the congregation. The groom stands near the head of the right aisle. The best man stands a step to his left and a step nearer the front pew.

As the soft prelude music fades, the opening strains of the wedding march swell forth, which signals the procession to enter. The bride's mother rises. The congregation follows her example. It remains standing until the clergyman gives the signal to be seated, which may occur when the bride and groom reach their places before him or after the betrothal is read or not until after the entire marriage service is completed.

THE PROCESSION

The bridesmaids and ushers are never paired with each other in the procession, though very often they are for the recessional march. If it has been decided to use the choir as part of the procession, it enters first, singing, followed by the rest of the bride's party in the following order:

1. Ushers, paired, the shortest leading
2. Junior ushers, paired
3. Junior bridesmaids, paired
4. Bridesmaids, singly or paired, the shortest first
5. Matron of honor
6. Maid of honor
7. Ring bearer
8. Flower girl
9. Bride on her father's right arm
10. Train bearers

The old-fashioned hesitation step is never used today for good reasons. It is jerky, unnatural, and extremely hard for the entire party to perform smoothly. The party walks in a stately, slow, but natural, gait. Usually a distance of four pews is maintained between each pair of ushers and bridesmaids, and a distance of six pews between individuals walking separately. Depending on the number of attendants and the length of the aisle, wider spacing may be allowed.

The attendants who are escorting the bride toward the bride-groom should fix their attention on him, not on the heels of the person ahead, the clergyman, or friends in the audience. It helps, too, if they remember to smile: Some attendants concentrate so much on keeping step to the music that their expressions look strained and not in keeping with the happy occasion.

There are many ways in which the attendants may be grouped during the marriage service, depending on the structure of the chancel, the arrangement of steps, and the location of the altar. The two arrangements most often seen are shown in the accompanying charts. In one, all the ushers line up on the groom's side and the bridesmaids take opposite positions on the bride's side. In the other, the paired ushers separate when they pass the front pews and take places right and left. The paired bridesmaids also separate and take places in front of them.

As the attendants reach their places, they pivot slowly and face the approaching bride, focusing their attention on her. When she reaches her place before the clergyman, they face toward him also, which brings them into a semiprofile position in relation to the congregation.

The groom steps forward as the bride and her father step in parallel to him. He then takes the final steps with her, placing them both directly in front of the clergyman. The best man advances to his place at the groom's right, one step behind him.

At this moment the organ music ceases.

The bride relinquishes her father's arm as the groom steps to her side. She transfers her bouquet to her left hand and either slips her right hand into the crook of the groom's arm, stands hand-in-hand with him, or simply stands beside him. This will have been decided previously at the rehearsal.

The bride's father remains on his daughter's left, one step back, until his part in the ceremony is completed. The maid of honor stands to his left, ready to move into the position opposite that of the best man when the bride's father retires to his place in the first pew.

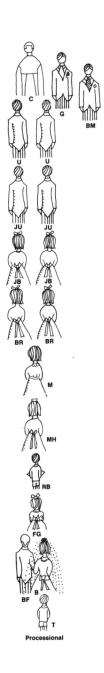

Processional

C = clergyman. G = groom. BM = best man. U = usher. JU = junior usher. JB = junior bridesmaid. BR = bridesmaid. M = matron of honor. MH = maid of honor. RB = ring bearer. FG = flower girl. BF = bride's father. B = bride. T = train bearer.

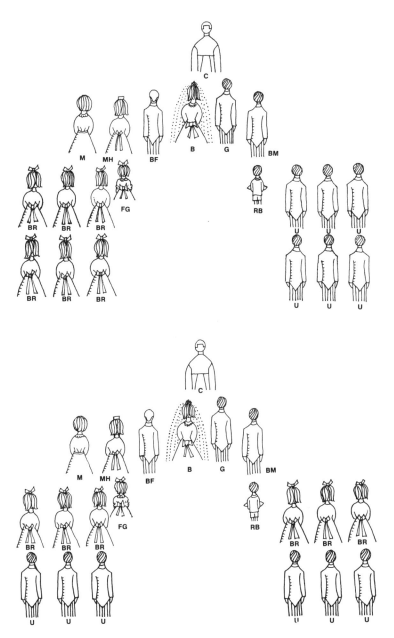

Above are the two arrangements for the beginning of the service that are most chosen. C = clergyman. B = bride. G = groom. BF = bride's father. BM = best man. MH = maid of honor. M = matron of honor. BR = bridesmaid. U = usher. RB = ring bearer. FG = flower girl.

THE WEDDING CEREMONY

There are two parts to the marriage ceremony: the betrothal and the exchange of vows, followed by the blessing of the union.

The father of the bride participates in the betrothal. When he hears the question "Who giveth this woman. . . ?" he steps to his daughter's side. She turns slightly toward him and gives him her right hand. In some ceremonies, the bride may kiss her father before giving him her hand, though it is not a standard part of the ritual. Her father then places her hand in that of the clergyman as he says "I do" or, sometimes, "Her mother and I do" and takes his place beside his wife in the first pew.

The clergyman, holding the bride's hand in his right, reaches out his left for the groom's and completes the betrothal by joining their hands.

There are a number of possible variants in the giving away of the bride. If her father is dead or cannot be present, the male relative chosen to escort her may answer "I do." Or he may make no response, and her mother may say "I do" without moving from her place in the front pew. In rare instances, the bride's mother walks beside her up the aisle. The bride does not hold her mother's arm as she would that of a male escort; they simply walk side by side. The mother stands beside her daughter during the reading of the betrothal, makes the response, and then takes her place in the first pew just as the bride's father would do if he were present.

Depending on the structure of the chancel and the location of the altar, the service may continue in the same place or the clergyman may turn and lead the way to the altar while the choir or a soloist sings or the organist plays.

At this point, the bride hands her bouquet to the maid of honor who has moved into the place vacated by the bride's father. If the service is to continue at the altar, the bride takes the bridegroom's arm and they follow the clergyman. The maid of honor has already given her own bouquet to the matron of honor or a bridesmaid so that her hands are free to receive the bride's flowers. She follows to the altar and stands a step to the left and behind the bride. The best man takes the place opposite her on the groom's right with the ring bearer.

The other attendants remain in their places while the marriage service continues with the exchange of vows, the giving of the ring or rings, and the benediction. In some ceremonies the couple partake of communion during this part of the service.

At the appointed time, the best man takes the ring from his waistcoat or his little finger or the ring bearer's pillow and hands it to the groom. He hands it to the clergyman who blesses it and returns it to the groom. He then places it on the third finger of the bride's left hand as he says the familiar words "With this ring I thee wed." (She has remembered, of course, to transfer her engagement ring to her right hand before the service. After the ceremony, she will return it to her left hand on top of her wedding ring.)

If it is a double-ring ceremony, the maid of honor produces the groom's ring. Or the bride and groom may each have been wearing the other's ring up to this point and exchange them after they have been blessed.

Following his blessing of their union, the clergyman congratulates the couple. He may shake hands, but even if he is a beloved relative, he does not kiss the bride at this point; the first kiss after the ceremony is always reserved for the groom.

The bride now turns slightly toward her maid of honor for her bouquet. She takes it in her right hand, even though her left hand may seem more convenient. Unless the bouquet is put in the bride's right hand, her left hand will not be free when she turns to take her husband's arm for the recessional.

If the bride is wearing a face veil, the maid of honor lifts it back after she gives her the bouquet. If the clergyman has approved, the bride may turn to the groom for a kiss at this time, though a kiss at the altar is not a part of the wedding ritual. It is not a usual procedure in the most formal of marriage services, though it is becoming increasingly prevalent today. A kiss immediately after the ceremony is customary at a home wedding or at the conclusion of a very simple ceremony, however, in order to ensure that the groom will get the first kiss.

The couple now is facing the congregation. The maid of honor adjusts the bride's train or long veil, if necessary, as the first strains of the recessional music swell joyously and the bride and groom start down the aisle.

The congregation rises at the beginning of the recessional music and remains standing until the last attendant has passed. All then resume their seats and wait for the ushers to return.

THE RECESSIONAL

The tempo of the recessional is not as deliberate as that of the processional; however, it is doubly effective if it is not rushed. Its pace and the spacing between the attendants should be as carefully rehearsed as that of the procession.

Sometimes the order of the procession is reversed for the recessional, as shown in Recessional A. In this case, the best man does not join in the exit march, but leaves through the vestry and joins the rest of the party at the main entrance.

More often, the order shown in Recessional B is chosen, since most brides prefer the symbolism of pairing their men and women attendants after the wedding.

EXIT OF THE CONGREGATION

Sometimes, after the last pair of attendants is about halfway down the aisle, the bride's father steps out of his pew, offers the bride's mother his arm, and they follow the bridal party as part of the recessional. The groom's father and mother follow the bride's parents by a few paces.

More often, the chief usher and another usher return up the center aisle immediately after reaching the vestibule. The chief usher escorts the bride's mother down the aisle with the bride's father following. The other usher waits until they are about halfway to the exit. He then offers his arm to the mother of the groom and they start out, followed by the groom's father.

The remaining ushers have walked up the side aisles so that they are in position to escort the other occupants of the reserved section. Sometimes only special or elderly relatives are escorted individually; in this case, the rest of the guests in the reserved section follow, pew by pew.

Not until the reserved sections are cleared are the ribbons enclosing the rest of the congregation released. Sometimes two ushers detach the ribbons from only two opposite pews at a time, starting at the front, and bow out the occupants of each successive pew. This plan leads to a very orderly and dignified parade of departure and also a more deliberate clearing of the church. This will be a definite advantage if most of the guests are going to the reception, since it will give the rest of the bridal party the time needed to assemble for the group picture and to form the receiving line. Otherwise, two ushers release the ribbons behind the reserved sections. Two other ushers, stationed at the rear, rapidly gather in the ribbons and leave them on a pew for the florist or the church janitor to collect later on.

RECEIVING LINE IN THE VESTIBULE

If the reception is to be small and informal or if there is to be no reception, it is customary to form a receiving line in the vestibule so that the newlywed pair can receive the congratulations and good wishes of friends who are not included in later plans.

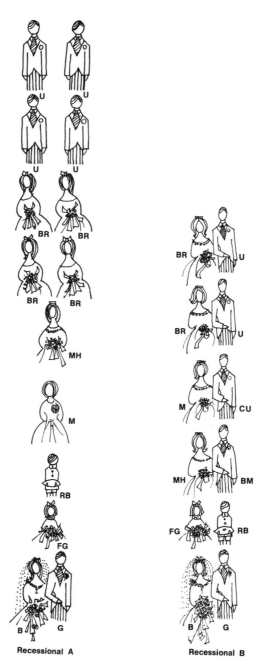

Recessional A

Recessional B

B = bride. G = groom. FG = flower girl. RB = ring bearer. MH = maid of honor. M = matron of honor. BM = best man. CU = chief usher. BR = bridesmaid. U = usher.

This receiving line is similar to that at any wedding reception. The bride's mother stands first. The groom's mother stands beside her. If the groom's father knows very few of the guests, he should stand next to his wife to facilitate introductions. Neither father is required to stand in this line. If they both choose to do so, the usual sequence is bride's mother, groom's father, groom's mother, and bride's father. The bride and groom stand next, she always on his right, and then the maid of honor and the bridesmaids.

A receiving line is never formed in the vestibule if a sizable reception is to be held elsewhere.

PROTESTANT EPISCOPAL WEDDINGS

A wedding in the Protestant Episcopal faith is generally the same as the basic Protestant ceremony, with the following exceptions and differences.

The bride is escorted up the aisle on her father's left arm instead of on his right.

It is usual for the congregation to remain standing during the service. They follow the example of the bride's mother who rises when the first notes of the procession music sound and does not sit down until the last person in the recessional march has passed her pew.

The bride's father does not speak in answer to the question "Who giveth this woman. . . ?" He signifies his consent by putting his daughter's hand into that of the clergyman and then joins his wife in the first pew.

Secular music is not permitted. A soloist is not usual, but the choir is often used, and a boys' choir is a singularly lovely part of many Episcopal weddings.

The bride and groom usually partake of Holy Communion together before the service unless the ceremony is to include a nuptial mass.

Episcopal marriages are held in church unless special permission is granted for the wedding to be held elsewhere.

One of the couple must have been baptized in the Protestant Episcopal faith. A divorced person may not be married in this faith except by special permission.

Roman Catholic Weddings

In the Roman Catholic faith, weddings are solemnized in church unless special permission is obtained to hold them elsewhere. A Catholic girl needs permission from her own priest to marry in another parish. If both the bride and groom are married outside their own parishes, they must arrange to have papers sent to the officiating priest showing that they are members of the faith in good standing. Banns (announcement of the intention of a couple to wed) are proclaimed in the parishes of both the bride and groom on three consecutive Sundays before the wedding.

One member of the couple must be a Roman Catholic in good standing before a priest may officiate, and the non-Catholic must meet certain requirements. A priest may not officiate at the marriage of a divorced person. A civil marriage, even if both parties are Catholic, is not recognized by the church.

The Catholic marriage service follows one of several established rituals, depending on whether a nuptial mass is included. A wedding without a mass may be held in the morning, afternoon, or evening. A wedding that includes a mass is scheduled before noon. A Low Mass lasts about thirty minutes; a High Mass, about forty minutes; and a Solemn High Mass, about an hour. The bridal couple usually partakes of communion during a nuptial mass. Catholic members of the bridal party may also receive communion, but generally the rest of the congregation does not.

It should be noted that many changes are being made in

Catholic wedding rites. Most of the rules given here have not been substantially changed, but because some regulations can be modified at the discretion of the ranking authority within a diocese, it is essential for an engaged couple to consult with their own priest.

Music must be sacred in character, but in some parishes the wedding marches by Wagner and Mendelssohn may be played with the priest's permission. A soloist may be used, and a choir is a beautiful, standard part of a formal Catholic service.

Usually the best man and the maid of honor are Catholic, but this is not a hard-and-fast rule. The bridesmaids and ushers are not required to be Catholic.

The bride's father escorts her up the aisle, but does not give her away. When he and his daughter reach the front pew, the groom steps to the bride's side. She relinquishes her father's arm and he moves back to the pew beside his wife while the bride and groom advance to the priest.

The procession follows the standard pattern given on page 196. Sometimes the entire wedding party goes within the altar rail for the second part of the service. In other ceremonies, only the bridal couple follows the priest into the sanctuary, with an acolyte, if needed, to help with the bride's train. In this case, the rest of the wedding party may be seated in special front pews while the nuptial mass is being celebrated.

In elaborate weddings, special mass books printed with the date and the names of the couple are presented to the guests so that they may follow the service and give the correct responses.

Non-Catholic guests are not required to cross themselves or speak the responses, but they are expected to lean forward when the congregation kneels and to rise when others do. Women guests are still expected to wear some kind of head covering when attending a Catholic service.

Eastern Orthodox Weddings

Among the churches in the Eastern rite are the Greek Orthodox, Russian Orthodox, and Eastern Orthodox. Their rituals and procedures are in many ways similar to those of the Roman Catholic church. However, their ranking authority is a patriarch; they do not acknowledge the pope as their spiritual leader.

Banns are proclaimed on three consecutive Sundays before the wedding. The procession and recessional are the same as in other Christian ceremonies, and the bride's father gives her away before he takes his place beside her mother.

The ceremony itself is dramatically different from other Christian ceremonies in several aspects. It is performed at a table, set close to the middle of the church, with candles, held by the bride and groom; flowers, wine, a Bible, and the gold crowns that will be worn by the couple (or held over their heads) during part of the service.

A good deal of the service is in Russian or Greek, depending on the denomination, of course. There is much emphasis on the number three, representing the Trinity. Two rings are used; the priest blesses each three times before placing them on the *right* hands of the bride and groom. The best man then exchanges the rings back and forth from the hands of the couple three times. Later in the ceremony, the priest binds the hands of the bride and groom together and leads them three times around the table. The service concludes with the choir chanting three times a traditional song, "Many Years."

The service lasts from one to two hours, and guests should be aware that not all Orthodox churches are equipped with pews. In some, chairs are provided only for the infirm; the rest of the congregation is required to stand, or kneel, from beginning to end.

The Wedding

JEWISH WEDDINGS

The three main divisions of the Jewish faith are Orthodox, Conservative, and Reform.

Orthodox and Conservative weddings follow long-established rituals that are quite different in some details from those used in Reform weddings, but there are many variations possible in all three divisions. Only the rabbi who will officiate can tell an engaged couple which procedures are approved in his congregation. Therefore, it is essential to discuss the details with him well in advance of the ceremony.

In general, the major differences are:

Orthodox and Conservative rabbis do not perform marriages between a Jew and a member of another faith, but Reform rabbis will officiate at what is known as a mixed marriage. After a non-Jew completes the required course of study and is accepted as a convert to Judaism, any rabbi may officiate in what is known as an intermarriage.

In Orthodox and Conservative congregations, the service is conducted almost entirely in Hebrew with several passages in Aramaic except in those states where the law requires that the marriage service, itself, be read in English. On occasion, part of the ceremony may be in Yiddish or in the native language of a foreign-born couple. In Reform ceremonies, the service is in English with a few blessings spoken in Hebrew. The cantor, who chants many of the Hebrew responses, officiates at the altar with the rabbi.

At Orthodox and Conservative services, all men wear a head covering—their own hats or the skull caps called yarmulkes. The latter are supplied at the entrance for guests who arrive without a head covering. Non-Jewish guests must wear them when they are offered. At Reform services, men usually wear hats, but in some congregations, they are not required to.

At all Jewish wedding ceremonies, men and women sit together. (In Orthodox congregations, men and women do sit in separate sections, but only during a regular religious service.)

The Orthodox bride is always veiled, and women attendants wear a head covering. The bride usually wears a face veil in a Conservative service. In a Reform service, she wears either a veil or other head covering, but her attendants sometimes do not wear headdresses, depending on the decision of the rabbi.

In Orthodox and Conservative weddings, the bride and groom usually are escorted up the aisle by both parents who stand up with them during the ceremony, but there can be many variations. Sometimes both fathers walk with the groom, and both mothers, with the bride. Sometimes the best man and groom walk side by side. The rabbi will tell you his preference in this matter. In a Reform wedding, the father of the bride escorts her up the aisle and then joins his wife who is already in place in the first pew. Her father does not give the bride away.

In Orthodox and Conservative synagogues and temples, the bride's section is to the *right* as one faces the Ark of the Covenant. Reform rabbis endorse the seating of guests described on page 188, with the bride's section on the left and the groom's on the right.

Orthodox, Conservative, and sometimes Reform weddings are held under a *huppah* ("canopy"). Made of cloth, often beautifully embroidered and decorated with flowers, it symbolizes the couple's new home. It is supported by four poles, either fixed in position or held in place over the couple and their attendants by four men. The rabbi, cantor, bride, groom, maid of honor, and best man stand under it. If it is sufficiently large, the parents of the bride and groom do also; otherwise they stand nearby to the right and left. A *huppah* is used at the wedding regardless of whether or not it takes place in a house of worship.

The rabbi takes a central place under the *huppah* with the cantor at his right. Beside or in front of the rabbi is a small table covered with a cloth. On it are one or two glasses of wine and a fragile glass wrapped in a napkin. The bridal couple stand in front of the rabbi, the bride on the groom's right. His parents stand to his left and her parents stand to her right. The best man stands a step behind to the left of the groom. The maid of honor takes an opposite position on the right.

The order of the Jewish wedding service can vary quite widely from congregation to congregation.

The usual sequence begins with a betrothal benediction during which the bride and groom sip from one cup of wine. The ring ceremony follows. In Orthodox and Conservative weddings, the ring is put on the bride's right index finger, which she later transfers to the ring finger of her left hand. This custom is not observed in Reform ceremonies.

The reading of the *ketubah* follows next. This is the written marriage document or "contract." In Reform congregations, the reading of the *ketubah* is optional.

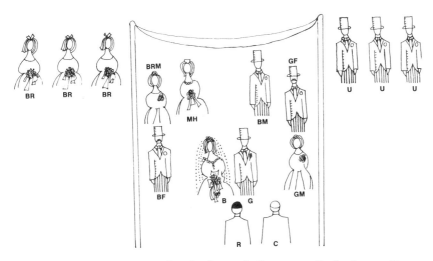

Standard positions under the *huppah* during an Orthodox or Conservative wedding. *C* = cantor. *R* = rabbi. *G* = groom. *B* = bride. *BM* = best man. *MH* = maid of honor. *GM* = groom's mother. *GF* = groom's father. *BF* = bride's father. *BRM* = bride's mother. *U* = usher. *BR* = bridesmaid.

211

After this reading is the chanting of the seven benedictions, and the bride and groom sip from the second cup of wine, after which the cloth-wrapped glass is crushed under the groom's heel. (The breaking of the glass symbolizes the destruction of the temple in Jerusalem which Jews must remember even in times of joy.) In Reform ceremonies, the breaking of the glass is optional.

The service usually includes a short address by the rabbi on the significance of marriage.

There are few restrictions on music used during the wedding ceremony. Secular music, such as popular show tunes and Israeli folk songs, may be chosen, though the bride and groom usually select traditional liturgical music or modern compositions that have been written expressly for weddings.

Receptions may be large or small, but they traditionally feature a blessing at the beginning of a meal and a benediction after it.

Jewish Procession

As noted earlier, many variations of the standard processional arrangement are possible. If the grandparents are to walk in the procession, the bride's follow the rabbi and cantor and the groom's follow the bride's. If the aisle is narrow, the parents precede their children. Sometimes the rabbi and cantor enter from a side door instead of leading the procession.

QUAKER WEDDINGS

The traditional Quaker wedding is simple yet quietly impressive. It may take place in a meeting house preceding a regular gathering for worship or in a private residence.

At least one of the couple must be a member of the Religious Society of Friends. A joint letter announcing their intention to wed is submitted by the couple to the society at least a month

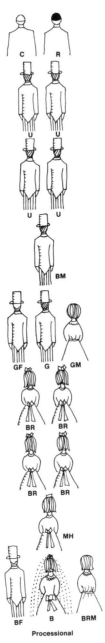

Processional

C = cantor. R = rabbi. U = usher. BM = best man. GF = groom's
father. G = groom. GM = groom's mother. BR = bridesmaid.
MH = maid of honor. BF = bride's father. B = bride. BRM =
bride's mother.

prior to their chosen wedding date. After the letter is read aloud at a regular monthly meeting, a committee of two men and two women is appointed to talk with the prospective bride and groom about the various aspects of marriage and its responsibilities. The committee's report is submitted at the next monthly meeting, and if all has gone well, there is a "clearness to proceed with marriage." Overseers are then selected to advise and help the young couple with the procedures of the wedding.

The bride may wear a wedding gown and veil if she chooses. The bride and groom may walk up the aisle together unescorted, or the bride may be escorted by her father.

The couple sit on a bench facing the meeting. After sitting in the customary Quaker silence of contemplation for a time, they rise and join hands.

The groom speaks his vows first, saying "In the presence of God, I take thee (her name) to be my wedded wife, promising with divine assistance to be unto thee a loving husband as long as we both shall live."

The bride then speaks her vows. No person proclaims them man and wife because, according to the Quaker faith, a marriage is created only by God.

After the vows are exchanged, the bride and groom sign a marriage certificate which the overseers must witness and which is often also signed by all others present. The certificate is officially registered just as any other marriage certificate is.

The main thing that a non-Quaker wedding guest must remember is that sometimes very long silences are part of a Quaker service. All present are expected to be completely quiet during such periods.

MORMON WEDDINGS

Members of the Church of Jesus Christ of Latter-day Saints are required to "live the law" of the Mormon health code before they may be married in a temple of the church by a member of the Holy Priesthood. The code calls for abstinence from coffee, tea, and alcohol and adherence to various other rules. Engaged couples who meet the requirements are married "for time and all eternity."

Non-Mormons should not feel slighted if they are not invited to the ceremony. Only Mormons in good standing are permitted to attend a wedding service in a temple; friends of any faith may be invited to the reception.

Mormons who do not qualify by "living the law" may be married in the faith, but not in a temple or by a member of the Holy Priesthood. A Mormon bishop or another person with the legal authority to conduct marriages officiates. Since such a marriage is considered a civil ceremony, friends of other faiths may be invited. The couple may be married later in a temple "for all eternity" when they have met the requirements of their faith.

CHRISTIAN SCIENCE WEDDINGS

The Church of Christ, Scientist is composed of laymen. Services for worship are conducted by readers who are elected by and from the membership, and there is no ordained clergy vested with the authority to perform marriage ceremonies.

Christian Scientists may be married by an ordained minister of any Protestant faith who will conduct a marriage service for those not affiliated with his own church. Or they may be married by a judge, justice of the peace, or other person legally authorized to officiate.

A Christian Scientist may marry someone of another faith. The wedding may be large and formal with many bridesmaids and ushers or very small and simple. In either case, the standard rules for Protestant weddings are followed.

Wedding in a Rectory

The simplest religious ceremony held away from home is the rectory wedding. It takes place in the living room or study of the clergyman's residence.

The bride and groom arrive together, perhaps with only their two witnesses. Sometimes members of the clergyman's family or staff serve as witnesses. Parents and a few close relatives may be present.

The bride may wear a wedding dress if she wishes, but she usually chooses to wear a pretty suit or dress with a hat or other head covering. She removes her gloves before the ceremony and lays them aside with her handbag.

The clergyman gives the principals a short briefing about their responses during the service before he begins to read the service. The bride and groom then take their places before him. Her father stands on her left only if he will give her away.

A large reception may follow or the group attending may accompany the bride and groom for refreshments at a restaurant or someone's house or the newlyweds may leave immediately on their honeymoon.

Civil Weddings

If a civil wedding is to be very simple, the bride and groom appear alone before a justice of the peace, with members of his staff or family serving as the two necessary witnesses. However, a civil marriage may be as elaborate as a formal wedding in church in the details of dress, number of attendants, and ceremonial bridal procession.

The Wedding

Informal Civil Weddings

If the marriage takes place in a city hall, another municipal building, or an office, the bride and groom wear street clothes. The bride may wear a pretty, modestly cut dress suitable to the time of day or a dressy suit, but she should never wear a classic wedding dress to a ceremony in business quarters. At most, there are two attendants: a maid or matron of honor and a best man. Usually only the parents and a few other relatives attend the ceremony.

A sizable reception may follow, or there may be a small gathering at a restaurant, hotel, or the home of the bride. If there is no reception, the bride and groom leave for their honeymoon immediately after the ceremony.

Semiformal and Formal Civil Weddings

When a civil wedding is held in a hotel, club, at a private residence, or in a garden, the bride may wear as formal a wedding gown as she chooses, with as many bridesmaids as she would like dressed to match. In this case, the groom, his best man, and the ushers dress with the same degree of formality. Though the bride's father does not give her away in a civil ceremony, he escorts her to her place beside the groom in front of the judge or other civil official conducting the ceremony. A civil marriage in private quarters follows all the details of any size wedding given at home. A reception always follows at the same location with refreshments appropriate to the time of day or evening. The usual receiving line is formed when there are many guests, and customary procedures are followed in the cutting of the cake, toasts, tossing of the bouquet, and sequence of the first dance. (See pp. 240–246)

Fees

There is a small fee for a registrar or similar official to perform the wedding. The groom may inquire by telephone what amount is expected. He or his best man hands it to the registrar in an envelope after the ceremony.

If a judge or other distinguished official performs the ceremony, a fee is not appropriate. Instead, a present suitable to the formality of the gathering is sent to his residence.

Religious Service Following a Civil Marriage

On occasion, a couple married by a civil authority decides to have a religious service later on, and they arrange to be married again in a house of worship. If a considerable amount of time has elapsed, the wedding and any party afterwards would be small. However, if the religious ceremony follows the civil ceremony within a few weeks, which sometimes happens when a couple is married away from their home community, there can be as many guests as the bride, groom, and their parents decide, and a regular large reception may follow. The bride does not wear a white wedding gown and veil, since these symbols of virginity are never appropriate to a second ceremony.

Home Weddings

A wedding at home has its own special charm whether the quarters are compact or very spacious and the ceremony conducted by a clergyman or a civil authority.

If the wedding and reception are informal and there are relatively few guests, the bride's mother greets them at the door. At a larger and more formal gathering, a maid opens the door, instructs the guests as to where to leave their coats, and the bride's mother welcomes them at the entrance of the room where the ceremony will be held.

The Wedding

The groom and best man usually wait elsewhere in the house or apartment and enter with the clergyman, either from a side room or up the aisle where the bride will enter a few minutes later on her father's arm. At a simpler ceremony, the bride and groom are present when the guests assemble. When the time comes, they simply take their places before the clergyman. They do not make an entrance together from a side room at a home ceremony.

The aisle can be marked in any convenient way—by placement of chairs or by ribbons or flower ropes looped on stanchions available from a florist.

Sometimes a few rows of chairs are provided for elderly relatives and friends; more often, all present remain standing.

If the ceremony is a religious one, a room in which the clergyman can put on his vestments will be needed. He will also need a substitute altar, such as a small table covered with a white cloth. This is a matter for the clergyman to decide.

Usually, the only attendants in a home wedding are a maid or matron of honor and a best man. If space allows, there may be bridesmaids and ushers. The ushers serve only in an honorary capacity, since the guests find their own places.

The bride's mother takes her place in the first row on the left. The clergyman, groom, and best man enter and take their places. If there are ushers, they lead the procession, followed by the bridesmaids, then the maid of honor, and the bride on her father's arm.

Immediately after the ceremony, the groom always kisses the bride. A receiving line is not formed unless the residence is so large that a reception can be held in another room or perhaps under a marquee set up in the garden. The bride and groom remain in place while guests come over to express their good wishes.

Music at a home wedding is often supplied by records, or a string quartet or other small musical unit may be hired.

The bride may wear a long formal wedding gown (without

a train) and a veil, if she wishes, or she may choose a much simpler costume.

Even if there is not going to be an elaborate reception, refreshments are always served following a wedding at home.

In a Borrowed Residence

If a relative or friend lends a couple a house for the wedding and reception, the rules explained on page 19 are followed.

In a Garden

All the rules for a home wedding apply to a wedding held in a garden. Of course, if the garden is quite large, the wedding may be more elaborate, since there will be room for a formal procession with many more attendants.

If there is to be dancing, a floor is set up, almost invariably under a marquee. Some sort of covering is always necessary as a safeguard against sudden changes in the weather.

DOUBLE WEDDINGS

Most often the brides in a double wedding are sisters. Sometimes the brides are cousins or intimate friends, although some faiths require that they be related. Occasionally, a double wedding is chosen because the grooms are brothers. The double ceremony, in addition to its inherent sentiment and charm, is exceedingly practical since the expenses for two separate weddings can be reduced.

Just as in any other wedding, the double wedding can be small and informal or large and very formal.

At an informal double wedding, each bride usually has her own maid of honor but no other attendants. Occasionally, each bride acts as the other's attendant, and each groom acts as the other's best man.

The Wedding

At any double wedding, each bride always has the same number of attendants, each groom has the same number of ushers, and all members of the bridal party are dressed compatibly; for example, the two grooms and their ushers all wear cutaways, dinner jackets, tails, or street suits. If each bride has her own set of bridesmaids, the girls' costumes should be the same length and similar in material and general style, although they do not have to be the same color. Often the bridesmaids and ushers are chosen together by the two couples; each bride, however, has her own maid of honor, ring bearer, and flower girl if she chooses.

If the brides are sisters, the older is automatically granted precedence in the procession, recessional march, and receiving line. She also is the first to speak her vows.

If the brides are cousins or friends, the simplest procedure is to give the precedence to the older. The matter of precedence is really not important except that it governs the seating of the two sets of parents and their positions in the receiving line.

The parents of the groom of the older bride sit in the aisle seats of the first row on the right. (The relative ages of the grooms have nothing to do with where their parents are seated.) The parents of the groom of the younger bride occupy the third and fourth seats in the first row, or they may take the aisle seats in the second row. The parents of the younger bride and of her groom are escorted to their seats first.

The same pattern is followed when the brides are not sisters. The mother of the older bride is the last one to be escorted to her seat.

The bridegrooms enter side by side, following the clergyman. They stand together, the groom of the older bride nearer the first pew, their best men behind them.

The Procession

If the brides are sisters, their father escorts the older, and the younger comes up the aisle on the arm of an uncle, brother, or other male relative. A father would never escort both daughters, one on each arm, up the aisle. The escort of the younger bride takes his seat as soon as she leaves him to join her groom. If the father is to give his daughters away, he remains at the left of the older girl until it is time for him to say "I do." Then he moves to the left of his other daughter to repeat that part of the ceremony. If the brides are not sisters, both fathers stand with them until it is time to give them away.

Two usual orders of the procession are:

1. Ushers of both bridegrooms, paired
2. Bridesmaids of the older bride, paired
3. Older bride's maid of honor
4. Older bride on her father's arm
5. Bridesmaids of the younger bride, paired
6. Younger bride's maid of honor
7. Younger bride on her escort's arm (a relative or her own father if the girls are not sisters)

or

1. All the ushers, paired
2. All the bridesmaids, paired
3. Older bride's maid of honor
4. Older bride on her father's arm
5. Younger bride's maid of honor
6. Younger bride on her escort's arm (relative or father)

The Service

The older bride and her groom stand towards the left before the clergyman; the younger bride and her groom, in line on the right.

Some clergymen prefer to read the entire service twice, but usually only those parts of the service that require responses are repeated.

The Wedding

The Recessional

The exit march is led by the couple first married, followed by the other couple, the two maids of honor paired with the best men, then the bridesmaids and the ushers, also paired with each other.

Receiving Lines

For sisters, the usual arrangement for a receiving line is:

1. Mother of the brides
2. Mother of the older daughter's husband
3. Older daughter
4. Her husband
5. Mother of the younger daughter's husband
6. Younger bride
7. Younger bride's husband
8. Older daughter's maid of honor
9. Younger daughter's maid of honor

Since the line is already long, the bridesmaids usually do not stand in line, though they may. For the same reason, the three fathers generally do not stand in line either.

If the brides are not sisters, two separate receiving lines are formed.

Both couples take the floor at the same time for the first dance, and the standard rules for cutting in are followed as closely as possible.

Each couple has its own wedding cake. The first slice of first one and then the other is cut so that attention will not be divided. The bouquets, however, may be tossed simultaneously.

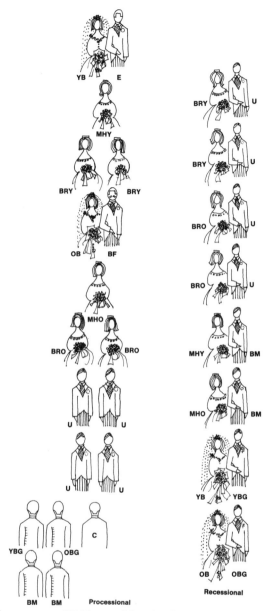

C = clergyman. *OBG* = older bride's groom. *YBG* = younger bride's groom. *BM* = best man. *U* = usher. *BRO* = bridesmaid, older bride. *MHO* = maid of honor, older bride. *OB* = older bride. *BF* = brides' father. *BRY* = bridesmaid, younger bride. *MHY* = maid of honor, younger bride. *YB* = younger bride. *E* = escort.

MILITARY WEDDINGS

There is no difference between the military and any other wedding except for the special "arch-of-steel" ceremony, a dramatic feature of a commissioned officer's wedding.

At the end of the wedding ceremony, the bride and groom remain in place facing the congregation while the ushers form two lines, facing each other, between them and the first pews. At the command of the head usher "Arch sabers!" (army) or "Draw swords!" (navy), they raise their blades, sharp edges up, points touching, to form an arch. The bride and groom begin the recessional march by passing under the weapons which are then sheathed. The ushers remain in place until the maid of honor and the bridesmaids have passed between them; then they follow, paired.

Some clergymen do not approve the unsheathing of weapons within a house of worship. In this case, the ushers leave by a side door immediately after the service is concluded and take position at the front entrance where they form the arch of steel. Only the bride and groom pass under the arched weapons, which are then sheathed.

The arch-of-steel ceremony is most effective when all ushers are in military uniform. If there are one or two civilians among the ushers, they line up with the rest and stand with hands at sides when the weapons are raised.

At the reception, the bride uses her husband's saber or sword to cut the first slice of cake.

SECOND MARRIAGES

The bride's marital status—she may be either a widow or divorcée—determines the character of a second wedding. Whether or not the groom has been previously married does not affect rules; however, if he has been very recently divorced or widowed, a quiet ceremony is in best taste even if it is the first marriage for the bride.

The bride who has been married before usually has a small, informal second wedding. She never wears a white wedding dress and veil or wears orange blossoms, which are symbols of virginity. Instead, she chooses a costume suitable to the hour of the ceremony and the formality of the reception. If she is quite young, she may carry a bouquet. More often, a widow or divorcée carries a prayer book or wears a corsage. The bride who has been married before is accompanied by one attendant but no bridesmaids. Her father may give her away if that is a regular part of the marriage service in her faith.

Decisions about the size and type of wedding and reception depend on many factors. If the bride was recently widowed or divorced, a quiet wedding and a small reception are preferable. If the bride's last marriage has been terminated for some time, a simple wedding and an elaborate reception can be a good choice, depending on her position in the community and that of the groom and whether there are children concerned.

The reception following a second marriage is basically like any other wedding reception. At a large gathering, a short receiving line is formed if the bride's parents are present; otherwise, the bride and groom receive together. The wedding cake is the same except that pastel colors are used in its decorations. The usual toasts are proposed by the best man. The standard sequence of the first dance is followed if possible. Since there are no bridesmaids, there is no real reason for the bride to toss her bouquet. If she is young enough to carry one and there are many young, single girls among the guests, she may wish to follow this custom anyway.

Children at Second Weddings

What is best for the children? This question must always be considered when plans for a second wedding are being made.

If the children of a divorced couple are deeply attached to both their parents and may in some way be disturbed by a remarriage, the best choice is to have a very small wedding from which the children are excluded. This is the standard rule for children of a divorced bride or groom, although the children may attend the reception. The decision rests with parents, not etiquette books. If the children would feel unhappy about being left out, they should be present.

The only rule still observed is that a child of a divorced bride or groom does not properly serve as an attendant. However, even this rule is broken if the divorce is of long standing, if the child has had little or no contact with the other parent for many years, and if the duty would be welcomed by the child.

The same rules apply to a widow, although her daughter may properly serve as her attendant (sometimes a little flower girl is her mother's only attendant) and a teenage or older son may escort her—if such duties will add to the child's feeling of security and happiness.

Parents of a First Husband or Wife

There are no rules governing wedding invitations from a widow to the parents of her first husband. This delicate decision is one that each bride must make for herself. If she is devoted to her first parents-in-law and if they approve of her decision to remarry, they may be hurt if they are not invited to the wedding and reception, especially if their grandchildren will be present. On the other hand, witnessing the remarriage of their son's widow may be a painful experience even if they fully approve of her decision to marry again. This is one of the reasons that guests at second marriages are often limited to immediate relatives and closest friends.

The same problem faces the widowed groom who has children; each couple must decide what is the most considerate procedure for all concerned.

ELOPEMENTS

An elopement is not always a surprise to the parents of the bride and groom, and it is not always the case in these marriages that strong parental objection has forced a young couple to "run away" for their wedding.

Not infrequently an elopement is planned with the approval of the parents as a practical solution to certain problems. In this case, the parents are informed of the plan, though not of the specific date.

For example, if an engaged girl's parents are divorced and not on speaking terms, and if she is deeply attached to both, an elopement may be the best way to avoid a wedding and reception where one parent is excluded.

Sometimes an elopement is the best way to avoid family controversy about where the wedding should be held and who should perform it when the parents of the couple are devout members of different faiths.

Often, the reasons are social and financial. The bride's parents may feel obligated because of their position in the community to give a very large reception if they give one at all. An elopement relieves them of this burden. Or, it may be that the bride and groom are dismayed at the prospect of an elaborate wedding which their parents would insist on and forestall those plans by eloping. A couple financing their own wedding may prefer to spend the money on something other than a large ceremony and reception.

Although it is true that an elopement is the most informal of weddings, it still has its formal rules.

Unless the marriage is to be kept completely secret for a

while, telephone calls should be made immediately after the ceremony first to the bride's parents, then to the groom's. The parents then spread the news in any way they please.

The bride's parents usually send engraved announcements within a month or so. The announcements, which follow the same form as those sent after any other wedding, give the date of the marriage and the city or town in which it took place. If the wedding was in a church, its name may be given, but otherwise the locale is not specified.

Very often, if the bride's parents want to show that family relations are not strained, they give a wedding reception when the couple returns from the honeymoon.

No one is obligated to send a wedding present following an elopement, but loving relatives and close friends usually send a token of their good wishes.

8

The Reception

Unless the reception is to be held in adjacent social rooms of a church or synagogue, the bride's car should be waiting in front of the main entrance as the newlywed couple emerges from the building. Ideally, the cars assigned to the rest of the bridal party will be lined up behind it. A reliable friend (not an usher who has other duties) should be delegated to deal with the traffic problem.

The most important consideration at this time is to get the entire wedding party to the place of the reception quickly so that the group picture can be made before the receiving line forms.

If the customary order of departure is followed, the best man helps each of the bride's attendants into her car and then assists the parents of the bride and groom into theirs. By this time the ushers should have completed releasing the ribbons and can leave with the best man for the reception.

Considerate guests who are going on to the reception find their cars or taxis leisurely in order to give the bridal party some extra time for posing for the group picture and for a glass of champagne before forming the receiving line.

The Reception

THE RECEIVING LINE

A receiving line is useful only at very large receptions. At small gatherings, the hostess, the mother of the bride, remains near the entrance to welcome guests on their arrival as she would do at any other party. If the groom's parents have not met many of the other guests, they may be asked to stand beside her so that she can make immediate introductions. Generally, it is more comfortable at a small reception if everyone is free to circulate.

A receiving line is a standard part of a large wedding reception, since it is the only efficient way for all the guests to extend good wishes individually to the bride and groom.

The receiving line may be set up so that the parents and the bride's party stand together, or else in two separate groups. The decision depends on making the best use of available space. The general sequence remains the same.

The bride's mother stands nearest the entrance with the groom's mother beside her. If the groom's father is in line, he stands third. The father of the bride generally does not stand in line, but remains free to move around and make introductions among his guests. If he does choose to stand in the line, the usual positions are bride's mother, groom's father, groom's mother, bride's father.

If the father of the bride is widowed or is giving the reception alone, he stands first in the line to welcome his guests. If he has remarried, his wife acts as hostess.

The bride stands on her husband's right even if this means that he precedes her in the line. It is usual to set up the receiving line on the left of the entrance so that guests reach the bride before the groom, but both sequences are correct.

The maid of honor stands third in this part of the line. If there is a matron of honor, she stands fourth. The bridesmaids, the tallest first, complete the line.

The best man, ushers, and child attendants never stand in a

receiving line; whether the bridesmaids do is optional. If the reception is exceedingly large and there are many bridesmaids, they may circulate among the guests while waiting for the line to break up.

In a formal receiving line, women keep their gloves on if they are part of their wedding outfits. Gloves are removed or tucked in at the wrist when the line breaks up. Women guests may wear their gloves until after they have gone through the line or they may remove them as they choose. Men always lay their gloves aside with their hats.

At a reception at home, or any informal reception, the mother of the bride does not wear gloves when greeting guests. The bride wears hers only if they are shoulder length.

Problems of Divorce

If the parents of the bride are divorced, but on friendly terms, they issue the invitations together, sponsor the wedding together (although they do not sit in the same pew), and each performs the standard duties of host and hostess at the reception.

Sometimes, if both parents have remarried, the mother gives the wedding and the father gives the reception. His new wife officiates as hostess, and if the bride's mother attends, she conducts herself as a guest. She does not stand in the receiving line or perform any other of the hostess's duties.

If the bride's father has not remarried and he gives the reception, the bride's mother may receive with him even if she has married again, but he stands first in line and she stands second to show that she is the acting, not the actual, hostess in his house. The same rules apply when the reception takes place in a club or hotel.

If the relations between the divorced parents are strained and the bride's mother gives both the wedding and reception, the father may appear at the ceremony but be excluded from the reception.

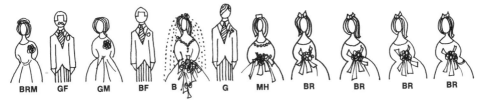

BRM = bride's mother. *GF* = groom's father. *GM* = groom's mother.
BF = bride's father. *B* = bride. *G* = groom. *MH* = maid of honor.
BR = bridesmaid.

Going Through the Receiving Line

The first duty of a guest when he arrives at a wedding reception is to go through the receiving line. It is not correct to by-pass a queue and get some refreshments, waiting until the line has shortened.

The guests should confine conversation to a few sentences at most; the receiving line is no place for a leisurely chat. (See p. 28 for rules about the use of the word *congratulations*.) If the guest is considerate, he will avoid fervently strong hand-clasps. The principals in a receiving line may be left with painfully sore right hands if they have to shake hands with dozens of people who mistakenly associate good wishes with a muscular grip.

When a man and woman arrive together, the woman precedes her escort along the line.

Introductions

It is likely that the hostess and the bride may forget even well-known names under the pressure of welcoming guests one right after the other. The considerate guest makes a point of stating his name if the hostess or bride do not use it immediately.

Men and single women identify themselves by first and last names without using a title. A married woman identifies herself by her husband's first and last name: *Mrs. John Grant.*

The hostess introduces each guest to the groom's mother. She repeats the name to her husband if he is standing beside her, or the guest restates his name to the groom's father, if that appears to be easier.

The same routine is followed when the guest reaches the bride's part of the line. The bride and groom identify strangers to each other, regardless of sex and age, since they are both guests of honor. When possible, some words of identification are added. The bride might say, "Dear, this is Mrs. Galt, who sent us the crystal fruit bowl," and the groom, recognizing an approaching friend, might say, "Darling, this is Mr. Burroughs, father's partner."

If the receiving line is exceptionally long, introductions can be dispensed with once the guest is past the bride and groom.

The Announcer

An announcer is necessary only at a very large reception if a great many of the guests are unknown or known slightly by the bride's mother. An announcer can be exceedingly useful when she will be required to greet by name and introduce many classmates of her daughter and new son-in-law and many business friends of both families.

The announcer may be a friend or a member of the caterer's staff. The announcer is not technically a part of the receiving line, though he stands between the entrance and the hostess. He occupies that position solely as her social aide. He smiles at any guests that he knows, but he does not offer his hand even to his good friends, and guests do not offer their hands to him. If he recognizes a guest, he turns towards the hostess and states the full name, always using a title: "Miss Marjorie Mc-Carthy," "Mrs. William Stetson," "Dr. Curtis Grant," and so on. If he does not recognize a guest, he asks, "Your name?" The guest states it complete with title. The announcer then repeats it to the hostess as she finishes shaking hands with the preceding guest. When a guest states his name, the announcer does not identify himself in return.

THE GUEST REGISTER

Many couples like to keep a special record of the reception guests as a souvenir. The most efficient way to collect all signatures is to post an usher or friend at the end of the receiving line with the guest book. If there is no receiving line, a bridesmaid or friend may circulate around the room with the book.

One member of a couple may sign for both—*Mr. and Mrs. Ernest Stafford* or *Emily and Ernest Stafford*—or each may sign separately. Men and single women do not use titles. A married woman who is not with her husband may sign her given and last name if she likes and if her friendship with the bride and groom is close.

REFRESHMENTS

The degree of formality of the wedding has little to do with the fare served at the reception. Simple refreshments, such as champagne or punch and wedding cake, may be served after an elaborate wedding or a full wedding breakfast, dinner, or supper dance may follow the simplest of wedding ceremonies.

Any party gets off to a good start if refreshments are promptly available. At a large reception, it is practical to station a waiter with a tray of filled glasses near the end of the receiving line so that guests can pick up a first drink without delay even if they must go to the bar later for refills.

The location of the bar deserves careful thought. It should not be too near the end of the receiving line because guests will inevitably cluster around it and form a traffic block. Some hostesses prefer to have all drinks served from trays by waiters. The expense for this extra staff is somewhat offset by the fact that consumption of drinks served in this fashion is likely to be less than from an open bar. Other hostesses prefer to use one or more bars so that guests can move around freely and will not form tight groups in one area.

It is always a good idea to have a sufficient number of waitresses circulating with trays of canapés rather than to depend on guests to find their own refreshments. At a simple reception, the bridesmaids can perform this duty, and young relatives of both sexes usually love this opportunity to help.

The type of food served at a reception depends on many factors—the hour, the time of year, the distance the guests have traveled, the local customs, and, of course, the budget. Caterers and banquet managers can be relied on to recommend menus that are practical for serving large groups; and there are countless cookbooks that specialize in menus and recipes for serving parties of all sizes.

Wedding Breakfasts

The wedding breakfast is actually a luncheon following a morning or midday wedding and is served at any hour from noon until two-thirty.

If guests are to be served at one table, there usually are three courses: a soup or other first course, a light main course, such as creamed chicken, lobster, or sweetbreads in patty shells; wedding cake; and coffee. Champagne or other wine is served throughout the meal.

If guests are to help themselves from a buffet, the first course is omitted. A buffet offers a great variety: a selection of hot casseroles or several fancy cold dishes, a choice of salads, and wedding cake. Simpler menus may, of course, be chosen: Many festive wedding "breakfasts" have featured cold cuts and potato salad with beer or punch.

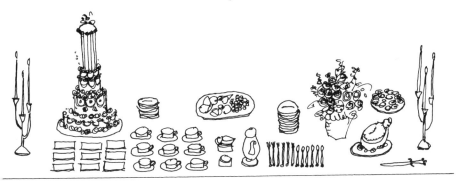

Afternoon Receptions

The dainty sandwiches and canapés suitable for a tea or cocktail party are the standard offering at an afternoon reception, with wedding cake, of course. Champagne is the traditional liquid refreshment, and it is customary to supply gin, vodka, Scotch, and bourbon for people who prefer these drinks to wine.

Dinner Receptions

A full-course dinner, whether a substantial buffet prepared at home or an elaborate meal supplied by a caterer or the banquet department of a club or hotel, is a major investment if many guests are invited.

However, if friends have traveled for some distance to attend a six o'clock wedding, it is only considerate to give them something more substantial than champagne and canapés. Here again, the range of menus is virtually limitless, ranging from a backyard buffet to a dinner in a private room at a hotel or club, depending on the size of the group.

THE BRIDE'S TABLE

A formally seated separate table for the bride, groom, and their attendants is customary only at a large reception at which a substantial meal will be served. If only light refreshments are served at a large reception, it is still a wise idea to reserve one large table which can be used by the bride, the groom, and their attendants as a base between dances. Since this table will seldom be fully occupied, place cards are not necessary.

The best arrangement for a formally seated bride's table is to have the wedding party seated along only one side of the long table so that they are all in full view. The bride and groom always sit side by side at a table of any shape, the bride seated to the right of her husband. The best man is on her right; the maid of honor, on the groom's left. The bridesmaids and ushers, as well as their husbands and wives if there is room, take the

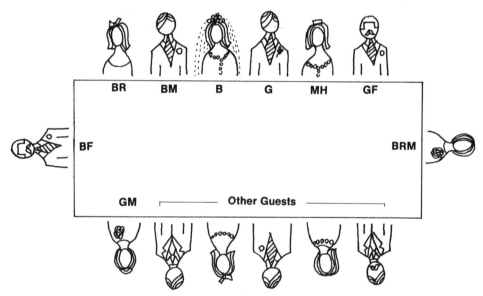

B = bride. G = groom. BM = best man. MH = maid of honor. BR = bridesmaid. BRM = bride's mother. BF = bride's father. GM = groom's mother. GF = groom's father.

remaining places, men and women alternating when possible. Place cards are needed for a formally seated bride's table.

A low flower arrangement makes the best centerpiece for the table. Sometimes the wedding cake is used as a centerpiece until the receiving line breaks up. The cake is then moved to its own small table to make cutting and serving easier, and either the bride and bridesmaids put their bouquets in its place or another centerpiece is substituted.

If the meal is a buffet, the bride, groom, and their attendants may serve themselves and carry their plates to the reserved table, but it is preferable to have that table served by waiters even if the rest of the service is less formal.

THE PARENTS' TABLE

It is not customary to set up a separate table for the parents unless there is also a separate bride's table. The father and mother of the bride, as host and hostess, sit at opposite ends of the parents' table. The mother of the groom sits at the host's

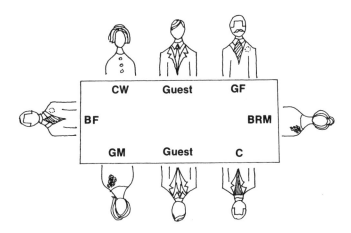

BRM = bride's mother. *BF* = bride's father. *GM* = groom's mother. *GF* = groom's father. *C* = clergyman. *CW* = clergyman's wife.

right and her husband sits at the right of the hostess. If the clergyman is present, he sits at the left of the bride's mother. The remaining seats are assigned to grandparents, and if there is room, to aunts, uncles, and godparents. Place cards are needed for a large group.

THE GUESTS' TABLES

If guests at a large reception are seated at several small tables for a meal, place cards are not used. Guests sit wherever they choose except at the tables reserved for the parents and the bride's party.

SEATING THE SMALL WEDDING BREAKFAST OR DINNER

If all guests are to be accommodated at one table with the bride, groom, and attendants, the bride and groom always sit side by side, the bride on his right.

If the bride's parents are not present, the bride and groom sit together at the head of the table, the maid of honor on the groom's left, the best man on the bride's right, and the other guests in the remaining places, men and women alternating.

If the parents are present, the bride's mother and father take the standard positions of host and hostess at opposite ends of the table with the groom's parents on their respective right sides. The bride and groom sit in the center of one of the long sides flanked by the best man and maid of honor; other guests fill in the remaining places.

DANCING

The time at which the dancing starts depends on the hour at which the reception began and on the size of the reception.

At a small reception, the receiving line will disband in less than half an hour; here, the long-established rule that no one dances until after the bride and groom have made the first turn around the room alone should be observed.

If the reception is large, the rule is frequently ignored, since it may take nearly an hour for all the guests to pass along the receiving line. The orchestra should be instructed to start the dance music before the line breaks up. This is preferable to keeping your guests standing around when they would rather be dancing. There is no reason not to break with tradition at this party if a change means more fun for everyone.

If dancing starts while the receiving line is in place, the "first dance" is staged later. The music breaks off for this. The best man and ushers cue the other dancers to clear the floor. The orchestra plays a short fanfare to call attention to the bride and groom as they take the floor alone.

After that, the customary sequence of the first dance is followed. Her father cuts in on the groom for a turn with his daughter, and the groom asks the bride's mother to dance.

The groom's father cuts in on the bride and her father, and the best man cuts in next.

In the meantime, the bride's father asks the groom's mother to dance. The groom cuts in on him, and the bride's father is then free to cut in on his wife.

After that, the bridesmaids and ushers join the others on the floor and remaining guests follow.

The first-dance sequence may appear more complicated than it actually is. A good way to ensure its success is to supply the groom, the two fathers, and the best man with cards showing the sequence of partners. These reminders can be handed out at the rehearsal with duplicates available at the reception.

The groom dances in turn with:

1. His bride
2. Her mother
3. His mother
4. The maid of honor

5. And at any time during the reception with each of the bridesmaids

The bride's father dances in turn with:

1. His daughter
2. The groom's mother
3. His wife

The groom's father dances in turn with:

1. The bride
2. The bride's mother
3. His wife

The best man dances in turn with:

1. The bride
2. The maid of honor
3. And at any time during the reception with both mothers and each of the bridesmaids

The Toasts

The traditional toast to the bride and groom may be offered at any time during a reception. If the entire party is seated at one table, the toast may be proposed when the first round of wine is served. An equally popular time is after the cake-cutting ceremony. The latter is the preferred time at a large reception, since the bridesmaids and ushers will have gathered around the cake table, and attention will be focused on the bride and groom.

The first toast is proposed by the best man. Even if he is a good speaker, he should keep his remarks short and serious. If the party is seated, he rises, catches everyone's attention, lifts his glass, and says something like: "To Mary Jane and John!

Every happiness in their life together." All present except the bride and groom rise, lift their glasses, and take a sip. A full glass should never be drained at a toast. Then everyone sits down, and the groom rises to say a few words of thanks for the good wishes and proposes a toast to the bride's parents. The bride and everyone except the recipients of the toast rise and join in drinking the second toast. The father of the bride offers a toast to the parents of the groom, and other toasts may follow. Toasts usually are proposed by men, but there is no rule that a woman may not do so.

THE CAKE

The traditional bride's cake is white with white icing. Pastel colors are often added in some of the decorations for the first-time bride, and they are always added for the bride who has been married before. A wedding cake may have only one layer, but the classic structure is two to five or more tiers, depending on the number to be served.

Sometimes tiny good-luck pieces of silver for the attendants are wrapped in wax paper and inserted in the bottom tier after the cake is baked. Their positions are marked by inconspicuous pieces of white ribbon or by some special detail of the icing so that slices containing souvenirs will be served to the attendants. The charms intended for the women are inserted on the left; those for the men, on the right.

The traditional shapes of the charms and their meanings are a ring: the next of your sex to marry; a heart: happiness in a new or current romance; a wishbone: a dearest wish will come true within a year; a coin: financial good fortune within a year. A dog for a man means that he will be single for another year, and a cat for a girl means the same. A thimble for a girl means that her industry and reliability will bring a great reward; dice for a man guarantee good luck.

The Groom's Cake

The tradition of having a groom's cake is not often observed today because of the expense of packaging. It is made of rich fruit cake, cut in small rectangles, wrapped in foil, and packed in tiny white boxes tied with white ribbon. The boxes usually are heaped on trays near the door, and each departing guest takes one as a souvenir.

If groom's cake is not provided, special small slices of the wedding cake are sometimes wrapped for the unmarried bridesmaids to take home to "dream on." As everyone knows, if a girl sleeps with a piece of wedding cake under her pillow, she will see the face of her future husband in her dreams that night. A thoughtful hostess has a good supply of suitable wrappings so that other single girls can also take home small pieces of cake.

Cutting the Cake

If a full meal is served, the cake is cut after the main course and served as dessert.

At a reception at which only light refreshments are offered, the cake usually is cut shortly before the bride and groom change to their going-away clothes. However, since there is no firm rule on this, the cake may be cut at any time during the party.

Sometimes the cake serves as a centerpiece on the bride's table or a big buffet table. These locations can present problems in cutting. The table may have to be disarranged and the cake moved to a place where the bride can reach it gracefully; it may also be difficult for a candid cameraman to maneuver around a big table to shoot the cutting of the first slice.

The best place for the cake is usually on its own small table, decorated with a long white cloth and a garland of flowers, which can be rolled into a central place when the time comes for everyone to gather around for the ceremonial first cuts.

The bride cuts the cake with a silver cake knife, usually with white ribbons tied to the handle. The groom helps her cut two slices from the bottom tier by placing his hand over hers. As a long-established ritual of good luck, he feeds her a piece of his slice and she feeds him a bite of hers.

At a very small party, the bride continues to cut pieces for everyone present. At a large gathering, after the first two slices are cut, a waiter or someone else takes over the task of "carving" the many-tiered cake.

Very often the tiny topmost tier is removed intact, carefully packaged, and frozen for the bride and groom to share on their first anniversary. The rest of the cake is cut, tier by tier, from the top. Since there are inserts of cardboard circles supporting each tier, which must be removed, the portioning of a very large cake is best done by an expert.

TOSSING THE BOUQUET

Just before the bride leaves the reception to change to her going-away costume, the bridesmaids are asked to gather for the tossing of the bouquet. Single girls may join the ring, though it is traditional that one of the bridesmaids be allowed to catch the bouquet if it is tossed anywhere within her reach.

The bride turns her back before tossing her flowers so that she will not seem to be aiming at any one girl. As everyone knows, the girl who catches the bouquet will be the next to marry.

Sometimes the bride wears a blue garter below her knee, and after she tosses the bouquet, she pulls up her skirt to display it. The groom removes the garter and tosses it to his ushers. The symbolism parallels that of catching the bouquet: The man who catches the garter will be the next in the group to go to the altar.

THE RECEPTION ENDS

All the bridesmaids and the mother of the bride may help the bride change to her traveling clothes or only the maid of honor and one bridesmaid may do so. The groom manages with the assistance of only his best man. Before the couple is ready to meet for their departure, a message is sent to all four parents to go to their dressing rooms for a quick private good-by. The bride and groom then meet at one appointed place from which they will start their traditional dash for the exit—though actually, they usually walk rapidly to their car instead.

The bridesmaids and ushers have previously passed around baskets of paper flower petals, and the guests toss the blossoms which represent a shower of good luck as the bride and groom run for their car. Rice has not gone out of style completely, but its inherent hazards account for its loss of popularity. If tossed with just a little too much vigor, the grains can sting painfully and inflict injury if they land in an eye; and they are so treacherous underfoot that the couple might easily fall.

Some couples are amused by signs chalked on their car and by cans and old shoes tied to its rear bumper, but most others would rather not have to deal with practical jokes. As their last service as a guard of honor for the groom, the ushers and best man should prevent unwelcome clowning and aid the couple in a fast, smooth departure.

The exit of the bride and groom is a signal for the party to end without undue delay, something that often escapes the memory of a few merrymakers.

RECEPTIONS ON CHURCH PREMISES

A family that takes an active part in the religious life of the community often decides to hold their reception in the social rooms of a church or synagogue. This also may be a good solution for the bride who prefers to avoid the expense of a reception at a hotel, club, or hall. A small charge will be made for use of the social rooms in a house of worship, but it will be minimal as compared to the rental fee for similar space elsewhere. There are also opportunities to cut down in other areas. Relatives and friends can easily help in providing and serving refreshments, saving the cost of a caterer's services.

Alcoholic beverages may be served in the social rooms of a synagogue, but most churches allow only nonalcoholic drinks.

THE DELAYED RECEPTION

A "wedding" reception may be held weeks or even months after a marriage that took place far from the bride's home community, for example, while she was at college or working in another city. When she returns with her husband, her parents may wish to hold a large reception to welcome both home and to introduce their new son-in-law to relatives and friends.

If the bridegroom is from the same community, the two families may decide to give the reception together. They are permitted to do this because the party is technically not a wedding reception, but a social event to honor and welcome their recently wed children.

A wedding cake can be a charming part of the refreshments. The cake would, of course, be white if it is celebrating a first marriage. Toasts to the health and happiness of the couple certainly are in order, but other special events of a wedding reception are eliminated.

Very often the parents of the groom give a similar reception when he brings his bride for a visit to their community.

Special rules govern the wording of invitations to delayed receptions. They are given on p. 159.

9

Essential for Success— a Good Check List

Organizing a wedding of even moderate size is a complicated production, and the only efficient way for the bride and her mother to deal with the formidable series of necessary arrangements is to work with a check list.

The following list includes the major steps, listed in a time sequence. However, since each wedding is different, you will have to adapt and expand or cut this list to suit your own needs. Just be sure to work with a plan that is organized on paper and to check off each item as you deal with it.

The bride and her mother will be responsible for making most of the arrangements and for reminding all participants of their special duties. Therefore the check list is directed to them, with specific exceptions. They may, of course, ask others to assist them. Some fathers, for example, enjoy taking an active part in the planning as do some grooms. The groom's parents, especially his mother, may also welcome the chance to help.

The items listed below should be taken care of three to six months before the wedding, depending on its size and degree of formality.

1. Determine the general character and size of the wedding and reception by working with the chart on pages 46 to 47. Be realistic when calculating expenses; costs will probably be higher than you estimate. This is the time to decide what compromises must be made to keep expenditures within your budget.

2. With the *groom,* choose the *approximate* wedding date. If both of you are employed, make sure that leaves of absence or vacation time will coincide.

3. If the wedding is to be in a house of worship, check with your clergyman's office to make sure that both he and the church premises will be available on your chosen date. Make a tentative reservation.

4. Make an appointment to call on the clergyman with your fiancé for a personal talk. (The *groom* makes the appointment if his clergyman is to officiate.) Make a firm reservation for the day and hour of the wedding as well as the time for the rehearsal.

5. Check with the clergyman's secretary about rental and service charges, fees for regular staff members, and the availability of equipment, such as canopy, aisle canvas, etc. Also inquire about regulations concerning decorations, music, and the costumes of the bride and bridesmaids.

6. If the reception is to be at home, make a firm reservation with a caterer if one is to be used. If the reception is to be held in a club, hotel, or hall, make a firm reservation for the room and the desired services.

7. Reserve a dance band or other musicians, especially if the wedding is set for a prime date; otherwise you may find that your first choices are already engaged. The same advice holds for the next three items.

8. Reserve the services of a florist if elaborate decorations are planned.

9. Reserve the time of a candid cameraman for the day of the wedding.

10. Reserve limousines if they are to be used to transport the bridal party to the ceremony and the reception.

11. Once the date and hour of the wedding has been confirmed, the bride can issue formal invitations to her attendants.

12. The *groom* issues invitations to his best man and ushers.

13. *Bride, groom,* and *both families* begin to compile the guest list. The *bride's mother* asks the groom and his parents to complete their lists by a specific date.

14. Set up a good bookkeeping system. Coordinate all lists to eliminate duplications.

15. Order the invitations and announcements. It is a good idea to order stationery for thank-you notes at the same time.

16. With the *groom,* begin looking for a house or apartment and the basic furniture you will need immediately.

17. Start shopping for the wedding dress, bridesmaids' costumes, and trousseau.

18. With the *groom,* choose luggage that matches or combines attractively if both need new sets.

19. The *mother of the bride* selects her costume and informs the mother of the groom of its color, fabric, length, and style.

20. Order the wedding gown. It should be finished six weeks before the wedding if your formal wedding portrait is to be sent to newspapers.

21. Make an appointment with the photographer for the wedding portrait.

22. With the *groom,* decide on color schemes for your kitchen, bath, and bedroom so that shower presents will be chosen in desired colors.

23. With the *groom,* make your final choice of silver, china, and crystal patterns.

24. Begin to address invitations.

25. Register your lists of desired gifts at stores before mailing invitations.

Two months before the wedding:

26. Complete shopping for your trousseau.
27. Order gifts for the bridesmaids and a gift (optional) for the groom.
28. The *groom* orders gifts for his best man and the ushers and his wedding present for his bride.
29. The *groom* or the *bride's parents*, as the case may be, places the order for the bride's bouquet and for all other flowers to be worn at the wedding.
30. Set up appointments for fittings of the bridesmaids' costumes.
31. The *groom* chooses a costume firm if formal clothes are to be rented. He or his best man notifies the ushers about fittings or makes sure that slips giving each man's measurements are filled out and returned to the costumer so that alterations can be made.
32. Make appointments for dental and medical check-ups. The *groom* does also.
33. Make an appointment with your hairdresser for the day before the wedding or arrange for hairdressing time at home on the wedding day.
34. The *groom* makes all necessary reservations for the wedding trip.
35. The *groom* makes final arrangements for securing a house or apartment and places the order for the basic furniture unless you are renting a furnished place.
36. The *groom* contacts a lawyer to construct a new will and an insurance agent to buy a new policy or to make changes in existing ones. You do the same.
37. Mail the invitations to arrive four weeks before the wedding, but not less than three weeks before that date.

The last four weeks before the wedding:

38. Send the formal wedding portrait and news release to the newspaper to arrive two weeks before the wedding.

39. Make reservations or other arrangements for housing your out-of-town attendants. The *groom* does the same for his best man and the ushers.

40. The *groom* takes you to select the wedding ring or rings if they have not been chosen earlier. Allow two weeks for engraving and delivery.

41. Set up a system for recording gifts, that is, a gift book. Keep it up to date.

42. Write as many thank-you notes as you possibly can each day.

43. The *groom's parents* make arrangements for the rehearsal dinner if they are to give it and issue the invitations. Otherwise, the bride's parents make the arrangements.

44. Make arrangements and issue invitations for your bridesmaids' luncheon or other party.

45. The *groom* or his best man makes arrangements and and issues invitations for the bachelor dinner if one is planned.

46. Check with the caterer or hotel or club manager about details for the reception, such as seating arrangements, placement of the wedding cake, the place to set up the receiving line, the parking of guests' cars, etc.

47. Give the florist final instructions about where your flowers are to be delivered.

48. Give musicians instructions about special numbers to be played during the ceremony and reception.

49. Continue to write thank-you notes.

50. Make final arrangements about where the bridesmaids will dress, their transportation to the ceremony, and where they will receive their bouquets. Give them a list of instructions.

51. The *groom* makes certain that the ushers receive similar instructions about the delivery of their costumes and boutonnieres.

52. Get the medical reports required for the marriage license from your doctor. The *groom* does the same.

53. If the wedding presents are to be displayed, have gift tables set up a week or more before the wedding. Take out a short-term floater policy to insure gifts.

54. Send out reserved-seat or pew cards or instruct special guests where they should sit.

55. Prepare lists for the ushers of guests who should receive special attention.

56. Address the announcements and have them ready to be mailed the day after the wedding.

57. The *groom* takes you to the city hall to get the marriage license about a week before the wedding, depending on local regulations.

The week before the wedding:

58. Change your name on all cards: subscriptions, charge accounts, etc.; and remember to change your driver's license and voter registration after the honeymoon.

59. Make a final check with all suppliers—florist, caterer, liquor dealer, musicians, photographer. Make out and deliver the place cards for the wedding breakfast or reception.

60. The *groom* makes a final check with the company supplying costumes.

61. Make a list of *everything* you will take on your wedding trip. Take a trial run at packing.

62. Have your own dress rehearsal, and check the time you need to dress for the wedding.

63. Assemble everything needed for the actual wedding rehearsal—stand-in bouquets, lists of guests for the ushers, first-dance reminder cards, envelopes with fees for the sexton, organist, and other such staff members.

64. Try to attend to numbers 58 to 63 a few days before the wedding and don't worry. Your wedding is certain to be a beautiful and memorable occasion.

Index

Index

Index

257

Index

for honor attendants' bouquets,
87
petals ,63, 67, 68
for the reception, 57, 86-87
stand-in bouquet, 181-182
tossing the bouquet, 246
Friends, telling plans to, 5
Furniture, 57-58, 95

Garden wedding, 78
Garnets, 13
Gift-givers, rules for, 122-123
Glassware, 57, 97, 98
Gloves
bride, 69-70
bridesmaids, 72
receiving line, 232
Good luck items, 70
Greek Orthodox weddings, 187, 208
Groom
adopted, 39-40
attendants, *see* Attendants
bride's present to, 109-110
clothing, 73-74
divorced, 39
expenses of, 54, 56, 57
legal change in the name of, 40
obligatory calls, 6
parents
invitations, 147
obligatory calls, 6
press announcements, 35
photograph of, 31-32
presents to attendants, 111
presents to the bride, 10-11, 109-
110
responsibility for living quarters,
57
widowed, 39
Groom's cake, 244
Guest lists, 126-127
Guest register, 235
Guests' tables, 240

Headdresses
bride, 70
bridesmaids, 72
guests, 76
Health insurance, 103
Health report, general, 92
Heirloom silver, 96-97
Heirloom wedding dress, 14
Home weddings, 218-220
Honeymoon, 54
cost of, 9, 58

Hotels
invitations to a wedding at, 141-
142
receptions, 80
Household trousseau, 57-58, 94-102
china, 57, 97
crystal, 98
furniture, 95
glassware, 57, 98
kitchen equipment, 57, 100-102
linen, 57, 98-100
silver, 57, 95-97

Impersonal announcements, 34
Initials
on linen, 99
on luggage, 93-94
on silver, 96-97
on trousseau items, 93
on wedding rings, 14
Inoculations, 81
Insurance, 103-104
consultation of the broker, 102,
103
life, 103-104
personal liability, 103
personal property, 103
travel, 103
Interfaith marriages, 50-51
Introductions
engagement parties, 24
receiving line, 233-234
Invitations, 125-172
acceptances to, 162-163, 166-167
admittance cards, 152, 153
announcement parties, 20-21
at-home cards, 153-154
to attendants, 60
by both families, 150
canceling, 17
ceremony cards, 159
church weddings, 141
club, 141-142
for delayed-reception, 159-160,
248
divorced bride, 146
divorced parents, 144-145
double weddings, 150-152
engraved, 130-133
envelopes for, 132-133, 135-140
addressing, 135-137
filling, 138-140
inner, 135
outer, 135-137
formal, 124-125, 160
groom's parents, 147

Index

Index

Index

Index